P9-EGM-133

SOCIAL MEDIA FOR WRITERS

Marketing Strategies for Building Your Audience and Selling Books

TEE MORRIS & PIP BALLANTINE

WRITER'S DIGEST BOOKS

WritersDigest.com
Cincinnati, Ohio

Distributed in Canada by Fraser Direct
100 Armstrong Avenue
Georgetown, Ontario, Canada L7G 5S4
Tel: (905) 877-4411

Distributed in the U.K. and Europe by F+W Media International
Brunel House, Newton Abbot, Devon, TQ12 4PU, England
Tel: (+44) 1626-323200, Fax: (+44) 1626-323319
E-mail: postmaster@davidandcharles.co.uk

Distributed in Australia by Capricorn Link
P.O. Box 704, Windsor, NSW 2756 Australia
Tel: (02) 4577-3555, Fax: (02) 4577-5288
E-mail: books@capricornlink.com.au

ISBN-13: 978-1-59963-926-0

Edited by Cris Freese
Designed by Alexis Brown
Production coordinated by Debbie Thomas

DEDICATION

To writers of all genres, of all backgrounds, everywhere. If you walk away from this book with a new idea for your social media strategy, mission accomplished.

ACKNOWLEDGMENTS

Social media has made an astounding impact on our lives, and we are reminded of this every day through Likes, retweets, and voice mails we receive from the platforms covered here. The inspiration behind this guide comes from the many questions we have received at conventions, at workshops, and even over a cup of coffee (or tea, in Pip's case); but this book currently in your hands would have never happened had it not been for Laurie McLean of Fuse Literary and the talents of Alex Rixey and Cristopher Freese at Writer's Digest Books. Thank you all for making things happen. A huge thank you, as well, to Chuck Wendig for our Foreword and all the authors who offered their own opinions, strategies, and best practices, making this book more about the community of authors who all came together to offer their own opinions on what works in social media. Social media, we know, is more than just a new marketing platform for authors, but it is a foundation for writing communities. This book has only reinforced that opinion.

ABOUT THE AUTHORS

TEE MORRIS has been writing science fiction, fantasy, horror, and nonfiction for over a decade. His first novel, *MOREVI: The Chronicles of Rafe & Askana*, was a nominee for the 2003 Eppie for Best Fantasy, and in 2005 the book became the first novel to be podcast in its entirety, ushering in a new age for authors. Following the podcast of *MOREVI*, he co-founded the audio literature hub Podiobooks.com with Evo Terra and Chris Miller, offering hours of original audio content from first-time writers and *New York Times* bestsellers in a podcast format. He then went on with Evo Terra to write *Podcasting for Dummies* (as well as the 2nd Edition alongside Chuck Tomasi). His expertise reached deeper into social media when he penned *All a Twitter* and *Sams Teach Yourself Twitter in 10 Minutes*.

In 2011, Tee returned to fiction with *Phoenix Rising*, the first novel in The Ministry of Peculiar Occurrences series, written alongside his wife, Pip Ballantine. The title went on to win the Airship Award for Best Steampunk Literature and become a finalist for Goodreads' Choice Awards for Best Science Fiction of 2011. Now on to their fourth book in the series, *The Diamond Conspiracy*, and the fourth season of *Tales from the Archives*, a podcast anthology featuring short stories set in their steampunk universe, the Ministry of Peculiar Occurrences series has won several awards including the Parsec Award for the best of science fiction podcasts and RT Reviews' Choice Awards.

Tee and Pip also host *The Shared Desk*, a podcast covering collaboration and other aspects of a writer's lifestyle. He now runs the social media initiatives for Stratford University located in Maryland and Virginia. Explore the works of Tee Morris, and his occasional geek rants, at TeeMorris.com.

PIP BALLANTINE started life in Wellington, New Zealand as a corporate librarian. Pip earned a Bachelor of Arts in English Literature and Political Science and then a Bachelor of Applied Science in Library and Information Science. Her first professional sale as a writer was a piece on the history of Wellington, written for *The Evening Post* in 1997. Since then she has gone on to produce both novel-length and short-form fiction.

In 2006, she became New Zealand's first podcast novelist with her debut fantasy novel, *Weaver's Web*. She went on to podcast three other novels and host her own slice-of-life podcast, *Whispers at the Edge*. Her podcasts have won both a Parsec Award as well as the Sir Julius Vogel award for excellence. Pip's first byline in the United States was *Geist* (Ace Books), launching the Books of the Order series. At the same time, she also wrote for Pyr Books Hunter, Fox and Kindred, and Wings, as well as co-writing *Phoenix Rising* with Tee Morris, the first novel in the award-winning steampunk spy series The Ministry of Peculiar Occurrences.

When it comes to nonfiction, Pip has been seen in *A Taste of True Blood* (Ben Bella Books) and worked behind the scenes as technical editor for *All a Twitter*. Pip's short stories have appeared in anthologies such as *Clockwork Fairy Tales* (Roc Books) and *Steampunk World* (Alliteration Ink).

She continues to co-author Ministry of Peculiar Occurrences series with Tee, as well as produce their award-winning podcast, *Tales from the Archives*, and co-host *The Shared Desk*. When not writing or podcasting, Philippa loves reading, gardening, and whenever possible, traveling. She is looked after by a mighty clowder of cats in Manassas, Virginia, with her husband Tee and their daughter.

TABLE OF CONTENTS

Foreword

You're a writer over here. And over there is the wide world of social media.

You've got your Faceyspaces, your Circlesquares, your Tinders, your Grindrs, your Blinders, your SexyPalFinders, your Bloobs and Gloobs and Innertubes. Okay, so only a few of these Seussian techno-monstrosities exist, but if I said Facebook and Twitter and Ello and Tsu, in five years they might not exist, either.

The point is, you've got this world out there. This connected world. This web of bridging threads that connects you, me, our phones, our computers, and probably soon enough, our refrigerators. It moves fast. The ground shifts under our feet daily.

On the one hand, social media is easy, right?

Get on it. Say hello. Say other stuff. Squawk into the void to see who's listening. (Spoiler alert: My refrigerator is listening and my refrigerator would very much like you to go pick up a six pack of beer. Dogfish 90-minute IPA, please.)

But then, what about that other side of it?

The *writerly* side. The *authorial* side.

I'm a writer. So are you, I'm guessing.

And you're wondering, how do I bridge those things? How do you tie together *you as a writer* and *you as a person on the social media thingies*? Is there value for you as a writer? Is there *danger* and *peril* for you as a writer? Yes to the first, and *hell yes* to the latter.

Can you tell stories on Twitter? (Yes.) Can you find an audience on social media? (Sure.) Can you burn your audience on the Internet? (Most definitely.) Can you sell books this way? (Yes, to a point, but please don't get spammy.) Do you *have* to sell books online and be all Author Person? (Nope.)

But how? How do you accomplish all of this? How do you keep up with what works and what doesn't? Don't different networks and services offer different ... well, networks and services? A value add here, a subtractive function there?

You need help.

And so, I've written this book—

* is handed a note *

Ah. Okay. Sorry. Turns out, I did ... not write this book? I didn't. Okay. Sorry. I write a lot of books and it all kind of blurs together.

I did not write this book.

Which is probably a good thing.

Because you need not just one Sherpa to lead you up this mountain of authorial social media enlightenment. You need, in fact, *two*.

And so, I give you: Philippa Ballantine and Tee Morris. They are going to hold your hand and take you on a tour of all of the weirdness and wonder that social media has to offer—and they're also going to helpfully point out the pitfalls, too.

Because boy howdy, are there pitfalls.

You wanna do this *I am an author on social media* thing right?

Then you need their help. You need this book.

Though, before you read any further, I'll offer my one piece of social media advice. Take it or leave it—hug it close like a dear friend, or discard it like an old sock.

That advice is: No matter what network you use, no matter whom you talk to, no matter the blog or the service or the size of your audience, be the best version of yourself online.

Don't be somebody else.

Don't be a sales machine.

Don't be an asshole.

Be a fountain, not a drain.

Be you, with all the *best stuff* dialed up to 11, and all the worst stuff shoved under the bed so that nobody can see it.

So endeth the lesson.

Now: Reach out and take Tee's and Philippa's hands. It's time to take a walk. It's time to take the tour. It's time to buy the ticket and take the ride.

See you online.

—Chuck Wendig, Author, Blogger, General Wiseass

"So what's your platform?"

This has become a common question that agents and editors ask writers, be they beginners or best-selling authors. Once upon a time— let's say back in 2007, which is several *generations* ago in Internet time—social media was considered a distraction to up-and-coming writers and a fad to the established wordsmiths.

Within a decade, that attitude has changed. Dramatically.

The beautiful thing about social media is that it's easy to pick up. It's designed in such a way that anybody can set up an account and get started. The problem is that writers and social media suffer a disconnect. That is, plenty of writers hate the notion of promoting their work. They simply don't want to be *that* snake oil–selling writer. And while they may feel very strongly about that, the reason authors must self-promote is a simple one: *If you do not talk about your book, no one else will.*

What complicates matters for writers, social media, and the relationship between the two is what happens when self-proclaimed introverts pick up a megaphone and blindly go about promoting into a void. As you might imagine, things can and do go horribly, horribly wrong.

That's where we come in.

We set out to write this book because we know lots of authors are struggling with the prominence of social media networks, managing posts, and their public image. Some are using social media in ways that make them look like a rank amateur. (Believe us, it's very easy to do.) You may read some of what we offer in this book and think, *Oh come on, that is common sense!* But some of that common sense sadly isn't as common as you would imagine. If you are new to social media, we'll show you some of the basics and strategies that go well beyond them as well. If you're an old hand at Facebook, Twitter, and Instagram, you can count on discovering something new to apply to your own social media strategy.

All this sounds very exciting, but right about now you might be wondering who this mystical *we* behind this book is. Who is leading you into this promised land of blog posts, podcasts, and status updates?

Together we are Pip Ballantine and Tee Morris, writers of the award-winning Ministry of Peculiar Occurrences steampunk series. Between the two of us, we offer more than two decades of experience as professional authors, published both independently and traditionally by New York publishers. In addition, Tee offers a decade of experience as a social media professional, having worked in corporate, government, higher and continuing education, and nonprofit positions. He also literally wrote the book, or in this case, *books*, on social media: *Podcasting for Dummies* and *All a Twitter*. Pip carries the distinction of being New Zealand's first podcasting author and has spoken on popular social media topics concerning authors both in her native country and the

United States. She remains the only winner of New Zealand's prestigious Sir Julius Vogel award for a podcast. This is who we are, and where we began our social media journeys, in 2005–2006, on the cutting edge.

Considering we predate the hipsters by at least a decade, you might accurately say that we are social media pioneers. (And Tee was drinking Dogfish Head beer before it was cool, you young, bearded whippersnappers.)

NOTES FROM THE MARGINS

Pip and Tee know a lot about social media, but it's always good to get several perspectives. Throughout this book you'll find notes, styled like this, highlighting professionals in the book business who have shared their thoughts on social media and their platforms.

We maintain blogs, produce podcasts, and work all the social media you will find here. Ours is a view from the trenches, and the strategies we offer for your consideration have won us critical acclaim and a variety of awards and accolades. What we hope you take away from this book is an understanding of and a strategy for social media.

Agents are increasingly looking for authors who are not only great writers, but who also have a solid social media presence. It's essential that authors take a strong hand in marketing their own books. Personally, I check out at least the Twitter and Facebook brands of every potential client I am interested in representing. If these writers also have a blog, and Instagram, Tumblr, or Pinterest accounts, I am even more impressed by them.

—LAURIE MCLEAN, FOUNDING PARTNER, FUSE LITERARY

You see, social media began innocently enough as a way for authors to extend their reach to readers on the Internet, and to connect on either a professional or personal level. Social media allowed authors to encourage others to write, or offered readers a peek behind the curtain at the creative process. This online outreach evolved into an essential part of a writer's life. Today, marketing via social media channels has become a necessary part of the author's skillset, as much as research, writing, and editing. However, since marketing or public relations is "someone else's job" in a writer's eyes, authors usually don't give it enough time and attention. When marketing and PR get moved to the back burner, authors make mistakes that negatively affect the book's audience and, possibly, their reputation. Most of these social media mishaps can be easily avoided. Others are stranger than fiction but are worth remembering and learning from.

Tapping into the potential of social media begins with understanding how all the tweets, updates, and posts began, and how authors should take the online environment seriously and maximize the tools available to them.

UNDERSTANDING SOCIAL MEDIA

To appreciate this weird and wonderful world of social media, it helps to step back to the early days of the Internet. If you don't remember that far back, here is a short refresher. Communication was one-sided; information was presented in a stationary, static format known as Hypertext Markup Language (HTML). HTML is the tagging system that is used to create Web pages to display text, images, and links. When you get to WordPress, you will be able to see this HTML code in the text viewing panel.

Here's an example of what it will look like:

> <em>Lost in the sea of social media? Don't know how to blog? Befuddled by Twitter? Faceblocked rather than Facebooked? We can fix that for you.</em>
>
> <h2><a href="http://www.onestopwritershop.com/wp-content/uploads/2014/02/tee_headshot1.jpg><img class="alignleft size-thumbnail wp-image-297" style="border: 0px none; margin: 15px;" src="http://www.onestopwritershop.com/wp-content/uploads/2014/02/tee_headshot1-150x150.jpg" alt="tee_headshot" width="150" height="150" /></a>Our Talent</h2>
>
> <em>Tee Morris, along with being an accomplished, award-winning author, has ten years of experience as a social media professional. He is also the author of four titles in social media and has spoken on

best practices coast-to-coast and around the world. Tee has worked for both nonprofits and corporations, and now his services can be yours.</em>

The basics of HTML still apply to current online communications (and we've found them very useful for tweaking our various blogs), but *interaction* with a site's topic or host is far different. That interaction is the primary difference between social media today and the very primitive forms of communication in the early days of the Internet.

BOOKMARK

Knowledge of HTML is not a necessity for using social media, but it is extremely helpful in some instances. The best thing about HTML is that it is easy to figure out and easier still to find online resources that will identify tags that will allow you to format text. It's a good skill to have under your belt.

First Forums, Which Begat Blogging

With the development of more powerful programming languages more interactive websites called *forums* appeared online. Forums granted their visitors the ability to interact with other visitors through threads of comments pertaining to topics started by the website's host or the site's community. Visitors to a forum subscribe to a site and then enter a username, profile, and any other personal details they wish to share with the community. Once subscribers find a discussion that piques their interest, they are offered an interface that allows them a voice in the conversation. Forum members can also introduce their own topics and subscribe to specific threads. They are notified through e-mail when new replies are posted. As they interact within the forum, they build a reputation within that site's community.

It was the programming language *RSS (Really Simple Syndication)* that truly changed the way we communicate online. RSS served as the foundation for a new kind of website called "Weblogs," or what people now commonly refer to as *blogs*. One difference is that a blog, as opposed to a forum, is hosted or written by one writer or a core group of writers. A blog's host is the only one allowed to post new topics of discussion. Subscribers and visitors can interact with the blog host via comments, but they cannot post new topics as they can in forums. Another major difference with blogs is that their content can be *syndicated* through other blogs. In syndication, segments of a blog post are shared on other blogs with links leading back to the original. This increases traffic for all blogs involved in the process. Topics previously confined to a host forum could be distributed through a vast network of blogs, commonly known as the *blogosphere*.

The blogosphere offered a more interactive way to communicate on the Internet, with new and constantly up-to-date information, the ability to cross-reference material, and a way to build an online community around an author and his books or series.

Proceeding with Podcasting

Blogging ascended to a higher form of communication in 2004 when RSS pioneer Dave Winer and former MTV VeeJay Adam Curry developed a new tag for the language—the *enclosure* tag—to allow blogs to syndicate more than just text and images. With an enclosure tag, a blog was able to distribute more robust media, such as audio and video files. Put simply, the tag provided a website address where the user could find these different types of files. It looks something like this in the HTML markup:

```
<enclosure url="http://onestopwritershop.com/file.mp3"
length="987654321" type="audio/mpeg" />
```

And thus *podcasting* was born.

Podcasting can be best described as "DVR meets the Internet," where after you subscribe to a podcast, episodes are stored on your computer or portable media player until you listen to or view it. Podcast media provides subscribers with full control, unlike audio or video webisodes, which are generally only available if you are connected to the Internet or tune in at a specific time. Podcasting offers a variety of programming that is yours to keep when you subscribe. For writers, it can provide an outlet to show the world your fiction by recording and releasing short stories or even your whole novel. Another option is to do an interview or chat show. We do both with *Tales from the Archives*[1] and *The Shared Desk.*[2]

The Rise of Social Networks

With the popularity of content delivered to computers via RSS, another form of data exchange emerged, offering subscribers a new, real-time method of connecting with others. No longer would writers have to attend a conference in order to "meet with" and learn from other writers and professionals in the business. Thanks to *social networking,* users control their communities and their connections. They can

---

1 www.ministryofpeculiaroccurrences.com/category/podcast/

2 http://www.theshareddesk.com

set up profiles in order to broaden professional contacts or even just to enjoy the company of fans and friends in the writing community.

Social networking sites exploded on the Internet, changing the way information is exchanged, how apps are developed, and how connections both of the professional and personal nature are made. With all the user-generated content available in text, audio, and video, social media has become the new wave of communications that anyone can use to their best benefit. It can be used strictly for purposes of free entertainment or it can be used as a powerful marking tool.

Though social media is widely used, there are still authors that get online simply because "someone told them to get online" and others who refuse to get online because it's a "diversion" they don't need.

Writing is a business. If you're a writer, it's time you take social media seriously and start seeing it as a business strategy for your work.

Book Marketing 101 (or Good Luck, You're on Your Own!)

One of the biggest myths people have about signing a book contract with a major publisher is that all you will need to do is write and that everything else—editing, marketing, layout—is someone else's job.

Not quite.

Editing and layout, most of the time, are handled by your publisher, but marketing usually falls on the author's to-do list. Occasionally publishers will spend some of the marketing dollars on new authors, but the majority is set aside for the major players: Patterson, Rowling, King, Steele. You know, the writers who don't need marketing.

Trying to understand how marketing resources are distributed can be best described with a quote from Shakespeare: "That way madness lies." No, it does not make sense, and as you should avoid Lovecraftian insanity, this means *you* need to take control of your book marketing. No one else is going to care quite as much about your book's success as you do. This does not mean you turn down assistance from your publisher if it is offered, but marketing is not someone else's job. It's part of your writing career.

And believe it or not, it's not as hard as you think.

FIND OUT WHEN YOUR BOOK IS SCHEDULED FOR RELEASE.
When you have a release date for your book, immediately go to a calendar and highlight that date. Then look at the month before and the month after. These two months are what we call your "full-court press" months for promotion. That's when you're going to want to focus your content on promotion. Too soon, and people will forget it by the time the book is available. Too long after the release, and people will get quickly bored with your platforms. It is possible to overpromote a title, so keep that in mind when you are planning out your heaviest promotions.

BEGIN BUILDING YOUR SOCIAL MEDIA CHANNELS if you have none or rejuvenating ones that are quiet months ahead of your book launch. A social media plan doesn't just happen with a wave of a hand and snap of the fingers. You need to start talking, start sharing. What you put out there does not always have to be about your book—it can be about you, the writer. What are you reading? How's your editing going? Blog posts, podcasts, and updates that relate to you, your writing, and related subjects matter to your community. Remember, it's about creating connections.

"A common mistake I see in submissions is the promise to create a social media platform once the book is published. In reality, this takes some time to do well and to pick up steam, and you can't rely on that happening within the initial shelf life of your book. I look for clients who already have a solid, brand-appropriate social media presence before I even pitch the book to publishers. With that in hand, they can hit their promotional stride at publication, rather than trying to scramble and play catch-up."

—GORDON WARNOCK, PARTNER, FUSE LITERARY
AGENCY; PUBLISHER, SHORT FUSE PUBLISHING

HAVE A PLAN FOR SOCIAL MEDIA AND YOUR BOOK. Now that you're building a network, start developing a strategy for your developing platform.

When preparing blog posts, what are the topics you want to cover?

What content is most relevant to your audience? Links on fashion? Steampunk? Science? Consider what you want to share with your audience.

What blogs would be most interested in working with you on tours, syndication of content, and guest posts? What about Twitter and Facebook parties? (We will get to these topics in chapters 4 and 5.)

Asking these kinds of questions helps you develop a plan around your book, making social media your outlet to reach out to your readers and fans.

STAY WITHIN YOUR BUDGET. When you start receiving your advance, consider the words award-winning author Robert J. Sawyer extended to his fellow authors: "Your advance is your marketing budget." This is where you're going to get funding for services like Mention or Sprout Social and giveaway items for Facebook and Twitter parties (which we will cover later in the book).

BOOKMARK

A quick and easy—but frowned upon—way to build your community quickly is to *purchase* Followers, Likes, retweets, and reposts through various third-party services. While doing so is a tempting way to build your numbers, it is never a good idea. Many of the "purchased followers" are nothing more than automated accounts (called bots) that post nonsense, links to porn sites, and other accounts. These links lead back to *malware* (applications that allow hackers full access to your networking platforms or even your computer). Also, the statistics are misleading. On the surface, you will have impressive numbers, but as these purchased follows are not genuine connections, your community will offer little to no engagement or interaction. While you do want the numbers, quality in your community is much more important than quantity.

When developing a marketing plan, it can be very helpful to talk to authors you meet at book events and conferences. Ask what platforms work best for them, what advantages and disadvantages they find for particular platforms, and how they manage their writing time versus time spent marketing via social media.

If authors you speak with talk about scheduling book signings as the best way to connect with readers, be gracious and give them your time. Then consider this reality check from us.

Old Dog: Why Book Signings Are No Longer Worthwhile

Before you assume that we don't like live appearances, let us say that this could not be further from the truth. We love attending book events, festivals, conferences, and, yes, book signings. We really do. They are a great chance to personally meet and shake the hands of people who are either new readers or longtime fans of our work. They are also great places to meet and network with our fellow authors—after all, writing can be a solitary pursuit.

Book signings, however, should never be your *entire* marketing strategy.

Bookstore signings tend to be more profitable for the *New York Times* best-selling heavy hitters, but for the average author it is a hit-or-miss venture, a roll of the dice that will either pay out or crap out. You have to consider the cost of your trip: Is this a local visit, or are you traveling out of town? Add to that the two hours you invest in actually sitting in the bookstore, hopefully signing books. If you are not moving books, then you are losing time. Calculate all these factors, and book signings get expensive in a different way.

Again, bookstore signings are not *bad*, but bookstore signings should not be your only strategy.

New Tricks: The Wonderful World of Content Marketing

When authors think about marketing, the overarching notion is that you need to "push your brand" because it is all about you. To a degree, yes: Marketing is about trumpeting your horn and talking about your worlds, words, and works. This is a very traditional approach to marketing, but in social media this kind of repetitive message gets old *very* quickly. Think about it: If every time you met with an author online he was talking about his books and that was *all* he talked about, how engaging would you find his conversations? In social media this is referred to as *signal-to-noise ratio,* and it relates to the quality of your statuses and updates. If you are constantly advertising or promoting something in your feed, your audience may tune out your updates as "noise." In doing so, readers may miss postings that they genuinely care about or can interact with, referred to as a *signal.* Signal is all about quality and what you deliver to your network. This is how a new method of marketing, called *content marketing,* has evolved into an effective strategy for online marketing, as content marketing is all about the strength of your signal.

If you provide your readers and fans with quality content, turning your various platforms into go-to sources for reliable information and fantastic media, you will establish a connection between you, your audience, and your work. People find your work through content related to it, i.e., by sharing websites, blog posts, and other media that is not yours but related to, in some way, your worlds. This is how you begin to build a reputation with other readers, book bloggers, and authors. An example of content marketing in action can be seen in our various *Ministry of Peculiar Occurrences* platforms. You can find them on Tumblr, Twitter, Pinterest, Google+, and Facebook. For every one post we offer that directly talks about our books, we offer really cool steampunk posts from blogs, podcasts, and websites other than our own. Sometimes it will be the post about our book that will garner traffic. Other times it will be a post from elsewhere on the Internet that catches the eye. We also offer the chance for other steampunk authors, artists, and creatives to appear on ÆtherFeature, a column that we run every Thursday about other writers and creatives in the steampunk world.

It may seem unusual to offer resources other than our own on our series' channels. Why are we offering these other resources time on our platform? After all, shouldn't we be marketing our books? Yes, the end result of marketing is promoting and selling our books, but by offering your platforms to others in your community (in the example of the *Ministry of Peculiar Occurrences*, it's the steampunk and science fiction communities), you reach your audience, and the audience of your guest contributors. What matters the most with content marketing is the quality of your content: Does your content resonate with your audience, and does it establish you as a reliable resource in your genre? By making your social media channels a soundboard for topics of interest, visitors to your site may want to know more about your work. Content marketing is promotion by example, and by establishing yourself as a solid resource, you can easily reach your readers. We dive deeper into the mechanics of content marketing in chapter 12.

WHAT YOU NEED TO MAKE THIS BOOK WORK

"I really don't have the time for this."

This is probably the biggest excuse we hear from authors on why they are not giving social media a fair shot. Where is this coming from? Could it be the productivity lost when weeding through the variety of Follow Requests on Twitter, trying to figure out which profiles are truly legitimate people and how many are simply spammers? Is it the several hundred invitations to the latest and greatest Facebook game that you have to ignore? Or how about on the blog you recently joined—is there a topic you feel compelled to write, and an hour later you are still working on that post? Whether it is approving others to follow you on Instagram or finding yourself drawn into a thread on Tumblr, the perceived investment of time in social media appears to be a common barrier.

Most authors know enough about social media to be dangerous, while others tend to have the wrong idea on how to manage it. What you need to make this book valuable, and to make social media work for you, is an open mind, time, and patience. Instead of tackling all of these platforms at once, select three and begin developing your strategy. The magic will not happen overnight—hence your need for time and patience. You will want to cultivate your online community, and eventually your audience will connect with you.

BOOKMARK

The most difficult part in writing any how-to book on technology is staying up to date with current events and developments after the book goes to press. This is why we are offering weekly articles and the occasional podcast (syndicated from TheSharedDesk.com) about social media for writers at our blog One-Stop Writer Shop[3]. Consider the blog and podcast your ongoing addendum to this book. Subscribe to the blog to stay in the know.

We want this book to be your trusted guide in navigating the various online platforms out there, and we want it to help you discover the best practices and strategies for you and how to make them work. We're here to help you, the writer, build a community around your readers and titles.

So let's begin.

---

3   http://www.onestopwritershop.com/blog/

Blogging has completely changed the way we consume content on the Internet. To truly appreciate this, you need to step back (if you are forty or older) in your memory to the early 1990s when the Internet was very one-sided in how it delivered content in a stationary, static format. HTML, after all, was just text. Sure, the text could be granted attributes. Pictures could be included with the right code, and if you *really* wanted to impress people, your website featured cute animated images or maybe an audio file that served as your website's soundtrack.

We call these years "The Dark Times" of website design. Younger generations call it "MySpace."

It was also customary to incorporate links that would take you from one location to another. If you wanted to become an *active* participant in a Web page's subject matter, you would find a Guestbook or a simple e-mail interface in a Contact Me/Us section where your comment, feedback, or criticism might reach someone. This was still static in its delivery method, but it was an opportunity, nonetheless, to interact with the site's host.

With the emergence of more powerful, versatile computer languages such as Active Server Pages (ASP) and PHP: Hypertext Preprocessor Web developers began experimenting with more dynamic websites where visitors could leave comments pertaining to topics started by the host, interact with one another in these various threads, and *subscribe* through e-mail to this online content, spreading the reach of the website. Around 2000, RSS took shape as the foundation for weblogs, commonly referred to as *blogs*. A blog is a platform made for a writer, usually written by one person or a core group of contributors, much like a website, but it can be not only subscribed to but also *syndicated* from one blog to another.

A blog provides the "home station" for writers. It's an author's website and a mechanism for broadcasting brand messages to "satellites," the social networks. Additionally, publishing blog content often, consistently, and in a focused manner makes sites more discoverable in search engines. For these reasons, it's imperative for writers to develop blogs based on the subjects about which they plan to write, about the books they have coming, and about the books they may write.

—NINA AMIR, BEST-SELLING AUTHOR OF *HOW TO BLOG A BOOK* AND *THE AUTHOR TRAINING MANUAL*

Perhaps the most useful innovation a blog offers is the way a website is updated instantaneously when new content is added. Instead of having to take a page off-line, edit it, test it, and then repost it, you either post or edit a page through a *GUI* (pronounced "gooey," and standing for *graphic user interface*) and make your changes. These updates are made live once you click the Publish or Update option. Instead of having to worry about how an update will affect the overall look of the page, the *template* you are using on your blog makes everything fit.

Blogs also offer their hosts the ability to notify their audiences of changes. Visitors to your blog are given the option to subscribe to your blog through an RSS reader like *CommaFeed*[1] or *Flipboard*.[2] Much like subscribing to a magazine, RSS delivers new content to readers' desktops, laptops, and portable media devices. The traffic is still counted and tracked, and your readership is kept informed while your site stays current and relevant.

BOOKMARK

If people are getting content delivered to them automatically, why have a website? Won't blogs detract from the current Web traffic? On the contrary, blogs can actually encourage traffic to

---

1 http://commafeed.com
2 http://flipboard.com

Web pages by offering links at the end of posts that take readers directly to the website, to other pertinent or relevant locations of your blog (if your blog is your website), or directly to "for more information" pages or additional contacts. Blogs and blog readers do not replace websites but work with them in order to promote traffic and nurture the community around them.

Blogging allows visitors the chance to interact with the blog's author, topic by topic, via the commenting function. Comments are open invitations to both guests and subscribers unless they are moderated. Moderators are useful to ward off spammers and to help "keep the peace" if the conversation gets too spirited. Blogs also offer the option to syndicate content by posting it on other blogs, thereby increasing traffic for both the host blog and blogs referencing the original content. Concepts, ideas, and resources previously confined to a single location can now be distributed through the *blogosphere*.

Blogging also keeps you writing, and that is a very good thing. To make blogging happen, you need a *blog engine* or a GUI that has been built for creating, posting, and managing content—and that blog engine should be WordPress.

WHY WORDPRESS?

A variety of blog engines can easily get you blogging in minutes. Just to name a few, you could use:

- LiveJournal
- Blogger
- MovableType

Each of these services goes about providing you your own personal blog in its own way. Our choice option, *WordPress*,[3] offers expandability in ways that other blog engines do not. First, there are a wide variety of *themes* to choose from. Developed by users for other users, these themes are free and easy to implement into your own blog. A

---

3 http://wordpress.com or http://wordpress.org

theme is a skin that defines all the design and layout for your blog. A fair number of them have the ability to be customized, but you are ultimately limited to what the creator allows you to do. You can also find custom-built themes—for a price—that will ensure your blog is a one-of-a-kind place. WordPress has earned a solid reputation within the blogosphere as a reliable and easy-to-implement platform for all of your blogging needs.

BOOKMARK

The difference between WordPress dot-com and Wordpress dot-org is expandability. WordPress.com is a fully contained package, offering a lot of plug-ins and options for free. However, you get more in the way of storage and options if you upgrade to WordPress's Premium services. WordPress.org offers thousands upon thousands of themes and impressive plug-ins, all designed and developed by WordPress users, that allow you to go beyond the basics. The trade-off with dot-org is that you download the WordPress software, install it, maintain it, and back up your blog *on your own*. To find out more about WordPress and working on it free of the dot-com restrictions, take a look at *Sams Teach Yourself WordPress 3 in 10 Minutes* by Chuck Tomasi and Kreg Steppe.

Producing Content

Understanding the WordPress interface is easy. If you can work a word processor, you know the WordPress GUI. The hard part is sticking with an editorial calendar. A blog without regular, consistent content does not represent a writer in the best light. It gets even harder to produce content if you are working on a deadline. After all, instead of blogging about writing, shouldn't you be *writing*? This is the common argument writers of all genres, of all backgrounds, have against blogging and its value. Truth is that, yes, your priority should be your commissions—those projects that come with editors, publishers, deadlines, and paychecks, and low on the priority list, along with other items pushed to the edge of your desk, sits your blog on the Internet, silently mocking you.

Blogging shouldn't be a chore or hindrance from your writing career. It is your best introduction to potential readers and your direct connection to your audience. With the right strategy, keeping your content lively, relevant, and consistent on your blog can easily fall into your writing routine.

With your first blog posts, focus on introducing yourself to readers and beginning to establish as someone with knowledge worth reading about and sharing. The actual promotion of your new blog, though, should not come until you have content within reach, polished, edited, and ready to schedule.

Here are a few ideas on blog topics:

- When I'm Not Writing (travel, interests, hobbies, or how you unplug and unwind)
- Authors Who Inspire Me
- Favorite Books (different genres, all-time, repeat reads)
- What Inspires My Writing
- Creating Characters You Love or Hate
- Software/Hardware for Writers (can also include productivity tips, research tools, etc.)

The above topics produce what is known as *evergreen content*. These blog posts can easily be rotated in and out of an editorial calendar in case something topical or breaking news (a new book contract, a news headline from the publishing industry) comes to your attention. Evergreen content can also be *repurposed*, which means roughly 60 to 80 percent of the blog post is tweaked, rewritten, and edited for guest postings on other blogs. The more posts you have like this on hand, the more content you have in case you find yourself running tight on time and short on blog topics. Before launching your blog, schedule five evergreen posts from this list.

Another approach to content that's commonly used and great for staying organized entails creating themes for different days of the week. "Monday Motivation" features your favorite motivational quotes from your favorite authors while "Tuesday Teasers" are selections from your upcoming book release or perhaps a work-in-progress closing in on completion. Themed days are great for simple, quick blog posts that are easily syndicated on other blogs and publicized on various social networks.

BOOKMARK

Another option for themed days is using an image as your post. For example, if you designate your Fridays as "Friday Funny," you can feature a humorous quote, either from a book or from an appearance, of an author you enjoy. With a graphic as a post, it can be easily featured on visual platforms like Instagram and Pinterest. Make sure the image you post is:

THERE ARE AUTHORS WHO TRULY LOATHE THE EDITING PROCESS, OR BELIEVE THEIR WORK IS SO DEAD-SOLID-PERFECT OUT OF THE BOX THAT EDITORS NEED NOT APPLY.

THIS IS YOUR FIRST WARNING SIGN, SPARKY – YOU NEED AN EDITOR.

WWW.TEEMORRIS.COM

- Formatted not as a portrait or landscape but in a perfect square. Instagram, in particular, features all pictures in equal ratios.
- Original photography or artwork created by you, or ...
- A royalty-free image that you have purchased. Use of copyrighted material, including imagery, without proper

permissions can land you in trouble if you're using it to promote your work.
- Branded with your website so when the image is shared others will know where it originates.

These images can be created in a variety of mobile and desktop applications such as InstaQuote or FontKiller 2. You will find out more about InstaQuote in Chapter 9.

A "sweet spot" to strive for with blog posts is between 500 and 1,000 words. It's okay if you go over that limit; but if you want to keep your topics tight and concise, this is a good target. Shorter blog posts are easier to consume and easier to create. Authors argue that they don't have the time to blog, but 500 to 1,000 words equates to an hour's worth of time. Tightening up your thoughts, proofreading for typos, and linking to relevant material in your post is another hour at the most. Within that range you can say a lot, produce a conversation, and still have time to work on your latest novel or short story.

Posting Frequency

So now that you have five blog posts on hand and maybe even a few images for those themed days, you've got content. You've got a blog. You've got an audience out there, just waiting to find you. How often should you post?

New bloggers often think of themselves as baseball players coming out of the batter's circle swinging two bats—only in the blogger's case it's two blog posts instead of two bats. Two posts a week that grab audiences with new content and fresh discussions potentially total 1,000 to 2,000 words a week. It sounds easy but is actually an ambitious plan when you break it down. First, this plan would burn through the evergreen content you created in the course of just one month. If you blink, you'll suddenly find yourself short on content.

How about we start with a less ambitious plan and just a few small steps?

Posting Weekly

When launching a blog, aim for weekly posts. Pick one day and make that your blog day. It can be difficult to maintain that schedule, and it could be a bit frustrating trying to build an audience when you are only posting once a week. The advantage, at least in the beginning, is you get a complete idea of what it is like to produce content for a blog on a regular basis. Weekly posting also allows you latitude to reschedule evergreen topics in light of topics you want to post in the moment.

If you choose to continue posting weekly, and provided you remain consistent and truly do post weekly—even when you're on deadline or really, really busy—you can cultivate an audience. So long as you can be patient with slow growth and development of your blog's audience, a weekly schedule may be the best way to establish a strong, confident foothold in the blogosphere.

Posting Twice a Week

You have been posting once a week, diligently, for a month or two, and you are scheduling any extra content you've managed to produce in between posts. You find yourself with a healthy backlog, and you are still finding yourself inspired to write a few new posts or post some images featuring motivational quotes or teasers.

Maybe it is time to think about upping your blog post frequency.

As stated earlier, posting twice a week translates into 1,000 to 2,000 words a week for your blog, an ambitious plan for a novice blogger. However, if you are inspired and you find yourself with a quickly growing backlog of content, two blog posts a week will work for you. An additional blog post a week can also help you build an audience faster, but keeping this audience means you must also keep the two-posts-a-week schedule running. Themed days can help in meeting your demand for content, as these posts, if visual, can be easily produced and quickly posted. Just as you did with your weekly posts, determine the two days of the week that work best for you.

The power of the blog was brought home to me when I had to go public about an unexpected delay on a highly anticipated book. I could have said, "I'm going to miss my deadline and I'm sorry," but instead I chose to write honestly about why the delay occurred and my own creative struggles. Readers were so decent and kind and patient with me. Twitter is fun, it's my favorite place to connect with other writers, my water cooler, and the best procrastination tool. But the blog is my venue to really write, and that is, in the end, what I do.

—GAIL CARRIGER, *NEW YORK TIMES* BEST-SELLING AUTHOR OF THE PARASOL PROTECTORATE AND THE CUSTARD PROTOCOL SERIES

Come up with five posts around your theme and then schedule them for a particular day. Provided the new posts are short enough (200 to 500 words), your turnaround on these themed posts can be even faster than for your official blogging day. With two posts a week, you should notice more engagement.

Posting Daily

So your backlog of content is looking solid. Rock solid. So rock solid that you consider just how awesome it would be to turn your blog into a machine of daily content. That would mean posting something new about your works, about your genre, about the writing industry every day, Monday through Friday.

Daily content for a writer's blog is bold, aspiring, and nothing less than impressive. Usually people who aim for daily content—even the ones who take the weekends off—tend to have staff on hand. Blogs with daily content also tend to have huge audiences, with readers who are ready and waiting for whatever news or trivia you have to share. This is why daily blogging is a commitment. A *big* commitment. As in *Titanic*-sized, Wagnerian-epic, Super-Size-That-Happy-Meal big commitment. Sure, there are shortcuts like the posting of original graphics and syndicating of other blog posts, but when you host a blog, your audience expects to receive content from you. If the majority of your content comes from elsewhere, you risk losing your audience to the sources you are syndicating. This is why syndication is terrific to have as an occasional treat. It's something new, something different. A blog entirely made up of syndicated content, though, is not what your audience wants. They want to hear your thoughts, your opinions, your voice. Your *original* content. If you are a writer of books, whether nonfiction or fiction, you have to consider that a daily blog will take up much of your time. And with all this time dedicated to blogging, when will you have time to write?

Daily blogging is a temptation, a temptation that tantalizes if you find yourself with plenty of content in your backlog. This posting frequency comes with many risks that you must consider before attempting such a schedule. Writing time is precious, especially when in the developing stages of a short story or novel. Dedicating yourself to a daily blogging schedule could cut into that precious time.

Whether you eventually decide on a weekly, biweekly, or daily schedule for your blog, consider the maximum amount of time you want to dedicate to content creation before you launch. Once you have a reasonable schedule, stick with your plan. As tempting as it may be to go beyond that budget, don't. This way, you can protect the writing time reserved for your works-in-progress.

BOOKMARK

On occasion we are asked about the value of blogging monthly. Is there any benefit in doing that?

Honestly, with bloggers of all backgrounds and professions dedicating themselves to weekly or biweekly schedules, people will probably pass on your monthly blog post in favor of the four blog posts found on another's site. Even twice monthly blog posts pale in comparison to an author's weekly blog.

If weekly is a schedule you cannot commit to, blogging may not be your thing. And that is okay. Better to meet the minimum commitment of a weekly blog post than to engage in an occasional blog post whenever you're moved by a whim. The time you could be blogging can always be dedicated to social media or another aspect of your career.

Taking That Tone: Finding Your Blog's Voice

Once you have your posting frequency decided, consider where your content will be coming from, as well as what "voice" you'll use for your blog. Blogging, after all, is not just an introduction of your work. Blogging provides a connection between you and your readers. What kind of connection do you want that to be? Professional to professional? Teacher to student? Person to person? Do you want to talk about what you write, how you write, how you live? Or perhaps all of the above? Blogs may look simple from the outside, but a lot of planning and preparation goes into them. This hard line of questions about what content you want to produce will serve as your foundation for the tone, feel, and voice. After that, it's your responsibility to create the content, keep up with the posting schedule, and provide a voice that will draw in new readers and keep faithful fans coming back to your website for more.

We have touched upon the importance of original content, but are you the last stop for content on your blog? You have been exposed to the idea of relying on the kindness of strangers, so let's take a deeper look at the content that comes from sources other than you.

Guest Bloggers

After blogging twice a week for some time, you will establish yourself as a source of regular, reliable content. Why not, then, reach out to other writers and offer them a place to share their thoughts? Invite other authors to write on topics you think your audience would enjoy, or let them take your blog for a day and speak their mind on topics they come up with but that you approve. Once a topic is agreed upon, schedule your guest or guests accordingly. Keep your guest posts within your word count parameters—500 to 1,000 words—and give them a day you don't normally post. Depending on how many people you want to offer a moment on your blog, you may have guest blog posts alternate with blogs of your own content. If you find yourself with *many* volunteers, step up the frequency and aim for a weekly feature of a new voice from your corner of the Internet.

Why would you want to invite other authors to blog? Guest blogging benefits both you and your guests on several levels. For you, your blog gets fresh, new content, a completely different voice, and a touch of variety. You also get the opportunity to introduce your blog to a new audience—your guest's. Your guests, on the other hand, are given the chance to introduce themselves and their work to your audience, so it's a win-win for everyone. It also allows guests to play the role of expert on whatever particular topic you have asked them to blog about. Finally, by appearing on a blog other than their own, guests increase their reach and in turn increase their search results, proving they are not exclusive to their own blog. You will learn more about improving search results in Chapter 11, where we talk about search engine optimization, or SEO.

Blog Tours

Another fantastic way of assuring content for your blog is to host a *blog tour*. Unlike a bookstore or conference/convention tour, a blog tour takes place in the comfort of your own home. Your travel itinerary consists of various stops across the blogosphere. On a blog tour, you guest post on other blogs, talking about your book and its relevant topics, all the while inviting the blog hosts to appear on your blog. This pay-it-forward approach to blogging and publicity is a great way to get your words in front of potential readers and to spread the word about your works.

You can get a blog tour rolling in two ways: Pay for someone to organize it, or do the work of organizing it yourself.

BOOKMARK

There are two kinds of blog tours. One kind of tour is just you hopping from blog to blog, as if you were traveling from bookstore to bookstore on a standard promotional tour. The other approach is to schedule a book tour between several authors and build a round robin of visits so that everyone in the tour

> visits everyone else's site. For a first-time tour, make a round robin with no more than eight authors.

Book bloggers who arrange blog tours for authors can earn a good amount of income. Price tags for these services vary, but one thing is certain: hiring a tour manager costs you the lowest in stress. Also, tour hosts usually know more bloggers and writers to approach than you do, making your investment a wise one.

You can put out the call to authors in your network, of course. This is probably the best approach for authors who have existing connections in the book industry. Using Google Docs or Microsoft Excel is the best way to keep track of participants and to schedule dates for your participants. Just remember: Whether hosting or participating, you are investing time and resources in keeping others and yourself on track. You do not want to miss an appearance or fail to produce a piece. People are relying on you for content, just as you are relying on others.

When your next stop on a blog tour comes up, your host may have interview questions already lined up for you, but sometimes you may have to come up with your own topic for a blog stop. This can occassionally be hard, especially if you are on a long blog tour and feel as if you cannot come up with another idea. Here are some to get you started:

- Who would you cast in the movie based on your book?
- What is your inspiration for this book?
- What is it about the setting for this book that you find compelling?
- Did you go deep into the motivations of your favorite character?
- Do you plot your novel, or are you a "panster"?
- What is your typical day as a writer?
- Who are your literary influences, and why?
- What lessons did you learn from working with an editor?
- Did you find your own voice and style in writing?
- What do you love about your cover?

These are reliable topics that hosts love to feature on blog tours. Pitch two or three of them to your upcoming stop and see what they want.

If they say, "It's up to you …," pick one and run with it. At the end of the tour, you will have a wider reach for your name and your work.

You will also have, at the end of the tour, new evergreen content ready for repurposing and posting on your own blog. Give your new content considerable time (at the very least, six months) from the end of the tour before you start posting it.

BOOKMARK

When you embark on a blog tour, do not write one post and then offer it as your entry for all the blogs where you intend to appear. Each stop is expecting unique content, and those readers following you while on tour will be sorely disappointed if you're saying the same thing over and over.

For the best practices to follow on a blog tour and other social media platforms, take a look at Chapter 13.

Syndicating Content

In the same way that podcasting is defined in a variety of ways (Chapter 3), bloggers tend to define *syndication* in different ways. For this book, we define *syndication* as taking the opening paragraph of another's blog post and featuring it on your own blog. You then add a link that reads, "To read the entire blog post, follow this link …" from your blog to the original blog post's origin. Syndicating a blog post provides your own blog content while directing traffic to another blog.

BOOKMARK

The optimal way to syndicate a blog post is to feature a post up to the point where the post's home blog breaks between two paragraphs using the "Read More …" attribute. The "Read More …" attribute creates a unique URL that picks up where the previous paragraph leaves off. Using this link you can have people start a blog post at one location and end at another.

While syndicating blogs is a great source of content, and a terrific way to encourage community between blogs in the process of sharing, syndication should happen only on occasion. Blog syndication should not be your only source of secondary content, and it should *never* be your sole source of content. As stated earlier, people are coming to your blog to hear *your* voice. Offering the voice of others is a fantastic way of inviting different points of view, but if your idea of blogging is nothing more than collecting the thoughts of others, readers may find themselves asking why they are coming to your website for any reason beyond picking up blogging resources that produce original content.

WordPress has a lot to offer for both the beginner and the experienced coder. With just a little investment of time to learn how it works you can create a strong foundation for all of your social media. In Chapter 11, we're going to build on this when we look at search engine optimization, and in Chapter 12 we're going to examine content marketing, which will give you ideas on how to populate your blog.

If this all seems too big for you, the good news is that there is another, smaller option! Consider the microblog of Tumblr.

Drive-By Blogging

The founder and CEO of Tumblr, David Karp, set out to make something less verbose and easier to handle than WordPress or other blogging platforms like Blogger. Even though he said that Tumblr was made for "those who don't like writing," that doesn't mean writers can't make the most out of this platform. In fact, it could be the most useful platform for those with limited time who still want to reach an engaged and youthful audience.

Tumblr might have started out as a way to do short-form blogging, but it has become huge itself—and quite popular, with over 94 *billion* posts.

The ease of use and the quickness with which users can share information make it attractive to a wide audience.

On Tumblr, users share all sorts of things they find interesting (such as images, audio, quotes, and short passages from books). They comment on posts, share, reblog, and build a community around their information.

When you first look at the stream of constant Tumblr information, it can be a little daunting. It flows through your feed like Twitter (see Chapter 5), but with more images, moving images, and videos. Your job is to put your information into the stream, but it has to be engaging and visually exciting to attract attention.

Some authors blog only with Tumblr instead of WordPress, while some use both. It's up to each individual to decide how much time she has available.

If you are short on time or find long-form blogging hard to get into, then Tumblr could be a good platform for you.

WHAT IS THE DIFFERENCE BETWEEN WORDPRESS AND TUMBLR?

If using WordPress is writing a letter to the world, then Tumblr is the postcard version: Tumblr blogs have a pretty picture and contain generally shorter posts about how your day has gone. Tumblr is also easier and quicker to read, and someone who views a post often shows it to other people. If you are lucky, the recipient will pin it onto his refrigerator … which, in this case, is another Tumblr account.

Deeper down, there are other differences, too.

While WordPress can either host your content or allow you to host it on your own site, Tumblr is more of a mash-up of a social network—think of it as WordPress and Twitter joining forces. The advantage Tumblr has over Twitter is that with Tumblr you have more than 140 characters to work with. So Tumblr allows you to show more of your personality than Twitter does. Make good use of this feature, because personality means a lot to those on Tumblr, but remember to *keep it brief.* Tumblr readers like to *scan* their feeds.

The other difference is that Tumblr is a stand-alone company, where as WordPress is open source. This means that a community of developers is free to work on WordPress, contribute to changes, and offer a variety of themes and plug-ins to broaden its capabilities. Tumblr allows the user some freedom, like personalizing his page, but it is not nearly as expansive as WordPress. This creates some restrictions in how you can organize and present content.

Tumblr offers a social aspect that WordPress does not. You can "like" and reblog posts, follow people who interest you, and make comments on posts, which is important in social media. *Interaction* on any network means people are taking notice of you, and better still, sharing your words with their audience. Interaction is what makes social media so much fun, as well as so different from the early days of the Internet. Sharing is not just caring it brings more eyeballs to what you are saying and, in turn, to your books.

Why Tumblr?

If you are a writer with limited time, Tumblr is a quick and easy way to share a variety of content. If you have a beautiful image to share or a snippet of audio from your work, then this is the place to be. There are plenty of eager eyeballs just waiting for it. The social aspect of Tumblr means you can connect with other readers and writers who share your interests. Building networks is one of the strengths of this platform; it's not just about posting your work.

If you want to use Tumblr as your main Web presence for blogging, you can also add pages. You might consider adding pages that detail your appearances or your biography, for instance.

In short, Tumblr gives you more space to work with than Twitter, and it is quicker and easier to fit into your day than WordPress. If you are not comfortable operating all the bells and whistles you get with WordPress, yet you want to have some measure of customization, then Tumblr could be a good option for you.

BOOKMARK

A great thing about social media is that you can enjoy the best of both worlds. There are WordPress plug-ins that will simultaneously create a post on Tumblr. The post is a selection of the opening paragraph, followed by the link that takes readers to the blog. It is not necessarily the same as posting original content on Tumblr, but it can assure you that content is reaching your Tumblr account.

So why not have your cake and eat it, too?

Wider Audience

Writers want to go where the readers are; and if you are looking for a young, engaged demographic, Tumblr is the place. According to Tumblr, 50 percent of its users are thirteen to thirty-four years old. So if your genre appeals to that demographic, it's time to jump into the Tumblr stream. Even if your readers are older, Tumbler has plenty of those users, too: 15 percent are over fifty-five. Tumblr is also different from most other social media sites in that it's pretty evenly divided between genders.[1]

While it may not be the biggest social media platform, one thing is certain: Tumblr readers are interested. They spend an average of fourteen minutes on the site, which is more than Facebook or Twitter users. So while there may be fewer eyeballs on the site, those eyeballs are there for longer, which gives you a better chance to impress.

Ease of Use

The Tumblr action bar makes it simple to use. Text, Photo, Quote, Link, Chat, Audio, and Video are options laid at your fingertips. You can upload your content directly from your website or another person's website, or you can just drag the image to upload it. Tumblr works hard to keep it easy.

Don't forget your Tumblr page and profile says a lot about you, so get in there immediately and customize it. Make this corner of the Internet your own. You can tweak the colors of your page or go for a theme that you can adjust to your style. The more original and unique your Tumblr presence, the more people will want to follow your blog. Many of Tumblr's customizations are offered as free choices, but there are some that you can pay for as well.

With Tumblr, you can also create a *group blog* where more than one person can post. You can assign members and then promote a few contributors (or all of them) to administrator (*admin*) roles, granting them the ability to invite new users, remove current ones, delete posts, and reply to messages. Regular members can add their own posts, as well as edit or delete them. Group Tumblrs are good if you are co-writing a book with another author, or if you are writing an anthology. However only *secondary* blogs (described in the next Bookmark) can be group blogs.

---

1 http://www.digitalinformationworld.com/2014/10/social-media-user-demographics-linkedin-tumblr-facebook-and-more-infographic.html

BOOKMARK

When you set up your Tumblr account, you establish a profile and your *primary* blog. The primary blog can be hosted only by the profile holder. Secondary blogs allow for multiple admins. Tumblr allows you to have as many secondary blogs as you desire, but your primary blog only allows for one administrator.

Another little time-saver is the bookmarklet.[2] Drag the bookmarklet into the toolbar of your browser, and whenever you see something interesting on a website, you can simply hit the bookmarklet. If you highlight accompanying text and then hit the button, that text will appear in a pop-up window without you having to do a thing. (Remember, Tumblr wants to make blogging as easy as possible.) You can then decide if you want it to appear as Text, Photo, Quote, Link, Chat, or Video. This nifty little device even grabs video and images. It also links back to the source but lets you add your own commentary.

The bookmarklet is a great time-saving device that allows you to quickly and easily share interesting items you find. And that's wonderful, because who doesn't love getting things done with less effort?

BOOKMARK

Readers cannot comment on your Tumblr blog, but if you install the third-party expansion Disqus,[3] then you can add that functionality. First, create a Disqus account, then click on the cog symbol on your Tumblr, and finally click on Edit Theme. Under Theme Options, enter the Disqus Shortname and click Save. Now your readers will have the option to comment, just like they do on WordPress.

---

2 https://www.tumblr.com/apps
3 https://disqus.com

Mobile Possibilities

Tumblr's app is available for all your smartphones—after all, Tumblr is about sharing and, in some instances, that means on the go. Readers love to see a slice of your life, especially if you are rubbing shoulders with other authors. The app offers all the features of the website optimized for your iPhone, Android, or tablet. Like all other social media platforms, it is up to you to decide how much you want to share. Rest assured, the Tumblr app is just as easy to use as its website sibling. If you want to take advantage of "Tumbling" while out in the wild, dive into the Tumblr app and keep your readers in the know.

BOOKMARK

WordPress is not the only platform that plays well with Tumblr. Many authors connect their Tumblr account to their Instagram account. You can easily sync your Tumblr from the Instagram app, just as you can for Twitter and Facebook. You will find out more about Instagram in Chapter 9, and you can learn how to sync up accounts by reading the Appendix.

What should you post to share with your readers?

- **TRAVEL.** If you're going somewhere interesting—even if it's just your morning walk—snap a picture and upload it.
- **FOOD.** Pictures of tasty things make for great Tumblr posts.
- **EVENTS.** Let people know you're accessible.
- **ARTWORK.** What inspires you? A steampunk fashion shoot? An iconic comic book panel? A classic piece from J.M.W. Turner or Georges Seurat? Post it!
- **ANIMATED GIFS.** We dare you to search Tumblr for animated GIFs of Tom Hiddleston. Go on. (Just make sure you have a few hours.) For fun, you can also look for author-related GIFs, like famous authors writing and pages turning.
- **PETS.** The Internet wasn't invented for animals, but sometimes it sure feels that way. Posting pics of your pooch shows your softer

side, plus it offers a bit of your personal life without using pictures of your children.

You might think these things don't apply to you, especially if you are just embarking on your writing career. But you'd be surprised how interested readers are in seeing inside a writer's life—even if you're a "new" writer. No matter how long you've been at it, it is good to establish yourself as a real person, not just a writing machine.

EXPRESSING YOURSELF: PRODUCING CONTENT

Photo and video content are the most reblogged and shared posts on Tumblr. They catch the eye and are more likely to stop readers who are scanning through posts. If you have posted something visual, you immediately have an advantage over the posts that are text only. Just be sure to link back to your website or other relevant material. Otherwise, you are wasting an opportunity.

Tumblr users also love *animated Graphic Interchange Format* images, or *animated GIFs*. Love them or loathe them, refer to them using a hard or soft *g* pronunciation, on this platform they rule, particularly if they feature pop culture. If you feel like spicing up your blog with GIFs, then you may want to check out the website Giphy.[4] There are plenty of wonderful, funny GIFs related to writing, writers, and beloved books, and Tumblr has a very active and passionate reading community.

However, unlike syndicating posts, Tumblr uses a feature called *reblog*. Returning to the Twitter and WordPress analogy, the reblog feature is the retweet of Tumblr. On a reblog, the post is re-created (with accreditation) on your Tumblr account and allows for likes and comments on your account. While reblogging is a wonderful feature of Tumblr and is highly encouraged, nothing beats original content. It's best to make your Tumblr a mix of both. For example, on our Tumblr blogs, we post original content with three reblogs in between. This strategy spreads out our own content while building that community feel.

---

4 http://giphy.com/categories

John Green,[5] author of *The Fault in Our Stars*, has a great combination of this. He posts information and insights about his books, but you also get a peek into his life, with pictures of what is happening in his world. You feel like you know this guy and you like him. Jami Attenberg[6] has a Tumblr that is mostly original content. It includes pictures of the world around her, snippets about what she is working on, daily observations of her life, and advice for writers. It is pretty dynamic. Kiera Cass,[7] author of the Selection series, posts all about boy bands and fun happenings with her series (lots of images, for example), and, best of all, answers questions from her fans. So if you hear other writers say writers aren't on Tumblr, that could not be further from the truth. Tumblr is a great place for writers to express and promote themselves, and have a bit of fun.

I use Tumblr as a coffee machine in my virtual office, as if it were a place to go hang out with others. I engage with fans with "Here's this cool thing I found..." kind of posts.

—ELIZABETH BEAR, AWARD-WINNING AUTHOR OF *KAREN MEMORY*

Don't forget to tag your original content, as this is the way others are going to find it. People search for particular tags that interest them in order to find new, interesting content. The Ministry podcasts we post to Tumblr, for example, are tagged with #steampunk #podcast #adventure #mystery. We can also add tags about any location in the podcast like #Berlin or #Ireland.

Blue Tags show posts that are being curated by someone in Tumblr itself. The #DIY in the image below is an example of such a tag.

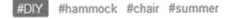

These tags mean you are getting free promotion for your post. Bear in mind that you can't make this featured tag yourself. You can only post great content and hope that one of the Tag Editors likes what you are doing. Tag Editors are chosen by Tumblr from the community, and

5 http://fishingboatproceeds.tumblr.com/

6 http://jamiatt.tumblr.com/

7 http://partylikeawordstar.tumblr.com/

they can change. They start off with a term of sixty days, and though some are invited to continue doing this job, others are not. So keep an eye on the tags to see what the current editor is looking for, but don't bend yourself out of shape to produce what they like.

Unique content is more likely to be picked by an editor, but a re-post of other people's content can be as well—but only if you have included the source information of where you got the image or post.

Finally, be sure to include as many tags as possible. Hashtags are your friend on Tumblr, like many other social media platforms. Popular tags include topics on fashion, vintage, film, makeup, and animals. So if you have any relevant posts, don't forget to tag them!

When producing content, you want to make use of Tumblr's best features: *Queue* and *Schedule*. Schedule lets you pick the time and day you want your post to go out. Queue grants you the ability to add a post to a collection of posts that will go out at set times. For example, you can adjust your settings to drop a fresh post from your queue once, twice, or as many times a day as you want. Tumblr also lets you set the time parameters of when you want the posts to happen. You can choose how often each of these posts from the queue fires off. Twice a day is a popular choice, but you can post into your queue up to fifty times a day if you want to—or are able to. We recommended two to five posts per day. Don't flood your feed, but don't leave it idle either.

Reblogging and Original Content: Which Is Best?

Though it's generally simpler than blogging, using Tumblr still requires a time commitment. There are writers who cue up original content or sync up their blogs with Tumblr in order to share their most recent posts in a feed, while other authors reblog the content of others and are happy with producing a highlight reel of all the "cool stuff" they've found on their own.

Reblogging others' content is a great way to build a community and display interesting items in your own feed. However, you also need to add your own commentary, so readers see you interacting with the post rather than mindlessly reblogging. If the comment ties the content into your own work as well, bonus points.

We want to stress that original content is not merely a link to "buy my book," though it can contain a link to buy.

BOOKMARK

There's an art to subtly advertising your book. You want to make it easy to find, but you don't want to hit people over the head with it either. Usually when we share images, we also include a short paragraph from the work, and below that a link to where people can buy it.

Original content can be pictures of your day, or observations of things around you, conventions or conferences, and people you meet. It can also be snippets from your published book or one you are working on. Tumblr readers want to learn something interesting and insightful about you and your writing.

WHAT TO EXPECT FROM THE TUMBLR COMMUNITY

To become part of the community, you need to make connections and participate. Standing on the sidelines simply doesn't make you friends. Don't be afraid to make the first move. When you first create your account, you need to find connections and start working on them immediately. Tumblr will suggest accounts for you to follow in the sidebar, basing its suggestions on the keywords you use to tag your content and the accounts you are currently following. Take a close look at what is suggested and start building your network right away.

BOOKMARK

A great place to start building your network is with the spotlights that are curated by Tumblr. Spotlights show the most interesting and popular blogs in different categories. Finding fellow writers is important so that you can tap into them.[8] Make sure you branch out into other interests you have, as well.

Don't worry. There are spotlights for all kinds of things: music, parenting, science, design, and many others.

Show your personality by following people outside the writing community. In this way, you can display what a well-rounded person you are. Readers are interested in people who write and what they do beyond the typing. Insights make you interesting.

Spotlights are not the only way to find the subject matters you're interested in. You can also look for blogs by doing a keyword search: travel, history, food. Tumblr features accounts on anything and everything. Tumblr lets you follow two hundred accounts a day, or five thousand different Tumblrs total for each Tumblr you manage. Don't be shy about following all you can. The more you follow, the more people will follow you in turn.

Don't forget to *like* (or *heart*) and reblog from your new connections—that way you are spreading the love and encouraging them to like and reblog your posts as well. When you start to get comments on your posts, be sure to respond to them.

Remember: Interaction is the key. You're cultivating a community.

SHARING WITH THE CLASS: SYNDICATING MEDIA

Sharing your information across various platforms makes for easy content. Since Tumblr has a different audience and community than other platforms, don't be afraid to repost content you are featuring on other locations, such as your blog, Instagram, or Facebook.

As you will find throughout this book and online, a variety of media, such as images and videos, will drive the most traffic to your content. If you are sharing something to look at or something to listen to, provided it is engaging, people will stop to watch or listen. The challenge is working within the limitations of Tumblr. Audio, for example, combined with a good cover image makes for great content. Our series The Ministry of Peculiar Occurrences has an award-winning

---

8   https://www.tumblr.com/spotlight/writers

podcast anthology, *Tales from the Archives*, and it gets coverage on Tumblr as well. However, in order to upload the content directly, the audio needs to be 10 MB maximum. Considering that the average short story we upload comes in at roughly 40 MB, it is not surprising that we have to remotely link such media. This material is said to be *syndicated* (a slightly different take on how you syndicate a blog post) back to Tumblr. When it comes to media, syndication allows for sharing of media beyond just Tumblr.

Different social media platforms have different demographics, and syndicating means you have the best chance of reaching all of them. It also can cut down on the amount of time you spend doing social media.

Avoiding a Potential Identity Crisis: Managing Accounts

You may have just one Tumblr account, but you are not limited to the number of secondary blogs. You can add up to ten Tumblr secondary accounts a day, but each additional account comes with limitations. Your secondary accounts cannot follow other blogs, create questions, like, or submit posts. However, secondary blogs can be great if you want to have a main author page and different Tumblrs for your different series (if you have them). For an author, having too many Tumblr blogs—especially if you are spreading yourself over other social networks—can be a way to (pardon the pun) tumble down the rabbit hole. Having a main author blog as your primary blog and then secondary blogs for a new series or characters from new titles is more manageable.

If you ever get confused as to which of your primary and secondary blogs you are working on, click on the head icon in the top bar, and it will show you.

TUMBLR STRATEGIES

Tumblr is all about sharing in the moment. Make the most of a mobile app and share images, quotes from your work, book trailers, and reviews—this keeps your feed interesting and helps build your list of followers. Keep your smartphone handy and make those moments immediate. In doing so, you give your fans a peek behind the curtain. If you are at a conference or a book signing, then post those images, but try to keep them fun. Take pictures of your table, your readers and other writers out on the town, or anything peculiar you find at the event. If you find some interesting cosplay (costume play), see excited readers with your books, or meet excited readers, post photos of them!

Create a connection with your community by sharing memes and news of interest to your readers. This can be about you or what is happening in the world around you.

As we've already said, video is popular on Tumblr, so if you have the time and skill to do it, then jump in. However, bear in mind shorter is better, and funny is even more engaging. You can record book reviews and chatter about what is happening with your own writing and the challenges you are facing.

Repurpose your blog posts from WordPress to reach the Tumblr audience. Keep them short and pithy, and don't forget to include an image to catch the eye.

Quote sections from your book and books you are reading to build interest. When building an audience using book reviews, you will draw more viewers to your site by talking about books that are similar to yours. This is particularly useful when preparing to launch a book. Tease the heck out of your audience with riveting or intriguing snippets from your work. Make sure you don't reveal anything too important, though! The idea is to create cliffhanger-type situations.

In general, the Tumblr audience in general enjoys visuals, so create images, videos, and GIFs to use. A riveting image combined with a concise piece of text does a great job of gaining attention and interest.

If you're sharing audio or a podcast episode, be sure to include an attractive image that's associated with it. If you (or your publisher) are releasing an audiobook, use samples and post them online. Don't forget to include the links to where they can buy it.

Use the Q&A function to engage with your audience. If no one asks you a question, post one yourself. It might be about inspiration for your writing, why a character acted in a certain way, or perhaps plans for more books.

Remember: If you are using Tumblr as your secondary Web presence, include a link back to your website in each post so readers know where to go if they're looking for more content.

Between WordPress and Tumblr, you have the basics of blogging available at your fingertips. Try both and get a feel for what works for you and where you think you will thrive. In the next chapter, we'll concentrate on ways to get your words and thoughts into your readers' ears. It's an exciting platform that delivers audio (and in some cases, video) directly to computers and portable devices around the world, and it's a lot of fun!

CHAPTER 3

Podcasting
Creating On-Demand Media Programs

With the many blogging sites, authors are able to get their words and inspirations out to readers. Instead of sharing those thoughts with written words, though, have you ever thought about sitting down and enjoying a fireside chat with your readers? That, in a nutshell, is what you're doing when you are *podcasting*. In 2004, programmers figured out how to use WordPress and other blog platforms to deliver dynamic content—specifically audio and video—to subscribers. Podcasters create their own media and syndicate it to listeners and viewers around the world. In doing so, they become a media production company, offering on-demand media content to subscribers via the Internet. These media files are consumed by subscribers through a host website, a computer's media player, or a preferred mobile device.

This is all well and good; however, many authors are not exactly dynamic in front of a microphone or a camera. Why would writers want to get into a media production platform when getting them to agree to public appearances of any kind is akin to moving mountains?

Perhaps the most obvious reason a writer would want to host her own podcast is because she has something to say.

BOOKMARK

Just because the FCC doesn't have jurisdiction over podcasts doesn't mean you're exempt from the law or immune to lawsuits. *You're personally responsible for anything you say, do, or condone on your show.* Additionally, the rules concerning airplay of licensed music, the distribution of copyrighted material, and the legalities of recording telephone conversations all apply. You still have control over the content you create, but make sure you obey the law.

WRITERS GONE WILD: TALK SHOWS

A podcast talk show starts with an idea, something that the creator has the desire and knowledge to fuel with his own voice. Add to that a bit of passion and a do-it-yourself approach to audio or video production, and the end result is a platform for whatever the author wants to say to listeners.

And writers can produce some wickedly fun content when the right people are in the room.

Podcast talk shows are like those you might find on television or radio. They are informal, off the cuff, and sometimes even involve guests. The topics of conversation do not always have to be about *the craft*, a topic *many* writing podcasts start off with. Podcasts we have produced in the past and that we have appeared on as guests have covered the following:

- Book Marketing (*The Survival Guide to Writing Fantasy*)
- World Building (*Serving Worlds*)
- Working in the Genre (*Adventures in Sci-Fi Publishing*)
- A Look into the Writer's Lifestyle (*The Shared Desk*)

These podcasts cover a variety of topics and also display the chatty, informal nature of the format.

These podcasts are a bit like sitting around with your favorite authors, enjoying a cup of tea or coffee (or, if the discussion gets really informal, a glass of wine or a beer) while they talk about whatever is on their minds or answer questions on a certain topic. Talk shows can be very easy to produce. Sometimes all that is required is a recording device and a topic of discussion.

There are two advantages to creating a simple talk show podcast.

- **MINIMAL EDITING:** It's just you and your guests, or just you on the mic, following a predetermined topic. You might have to edit the occasional stumble or tangent, but generally the talk show format is one of the easiest to produce. Without the need for heavy editing, it shouldn't take much time to clean up and produce an episode. You will want to review the recording for quality and flow, of course, but sometimes you can record, edit, review, and post all in one night.

- **MINIMAL PRODUCTION:** Along with editing, quality concerns such as background noise (which can add to the spontaneity of the show, especially if you have cats) are taken lightly. The talk show is more about a slice of life or a casual sit-down with literary professionals. Your main priority should be that everyone is clearly heard. Preplanning for production can be a bullet list of talking points, while your post-production should be creating *show notes* during the review process. Show notes accompanying the episode's blog post give listeners an idea of what happens during the show. It also helps if they want to skip ahead to a specific portion or find websites you might have mentioned. Links back to these sites are always appreciated by the websites' hosts.

The biggest benefit of the talk show format is allowing your readers to get to know you, see how your creative mind works, and enjoy a sit-down with you and your guests. Making that personal connection can go a long way in social media.

ANTHOLOGIES IN AUDIO: SHORT STORIES

Thanks to podcasting and its pioneers, like Mur Lafferty and Patrick E. McLean, short stories are enjoying a renaissance. Shows like *Escape Pod, The Voice of Free Planet X,* and *The Melting Potcast* all feature short stories as part of their programming. Depending on your posting schedule, short fiction podcasts can be demanding, but they are a great way to introduce yourself, your work, and your world to a new audience.

We produce the Parsec-winning podcast *Tales from the Archives*, in its fourth season at the time of this book's publication. The seasonal anthology, delivering new short story audio on a biweekly schedule, is set in the world of The Ministry of Peculiar Occurrences, our award-winning steampunk series. For this production, we have scaled down our production time considerably by approaching the podcast with this strategy:

- **STORIES READ BY THE AUTHOR:** Each season of *Tales from the Archives* offers ten to twelve stories, only two written by us. The remaining short stories are written and read by authors we invite to write in our universe. To do this, we offer guidelines, editorial passes on the manuscript, and post-production services on their audio. The lion's share of the work is in the writing, recording, and editing of the short story, all of which falls to the author.
- **POST-PRODUCTION PROCESS:** Once we receive an author's short story, we review the audio and then score the stories with a soundtrack and, if time allows, a few sound effects for key moments. These production elements bring an added dimension to the stories and are choices we make as content producers in an effort to do something different, something inspired.

BOOKMARK

It is totally up to you whether you want to do a straight read or go even further with sound effects and music. Any elements you add into your podcasting anthology—sound effects, music, guest voices—lengthens your production time. At the very least, if you are working with audio from other authors, you will want to teach yourself how to use audio filters to sweeten the clarity and quality of your guests' audio.

- **BIWEEKLY POSTING SCHEDULE:** As with blogging, a monthly schedule for podcasting tends not to be frequent enough to keep listeners engaged, while a weekly schedule consumes free time like children rummaging through their Halloween candy score.

A biweekly schedule, however, serves as a comfortable compromise, allowing time to produce and edit another episode while also developing new material and keeping with present editorial commitments. For all podcasts, a biweekly schedule is the easiest to keep and maintain.

GOING ALL IN: PODCAST NOVELS

In January 2005, Tee came up with a premise that—at the time—podcasters regarded as mighty ambitious: podcasting a novel from cover to cover. With *The Dragon Page* podcast hosting, Tee's trailblazing was followed by young adult author Mark Jeffrey and science fiction and horror novelist Scott Sigler. In the decade that followed, writers like Mur Lafferty, P.G. Holyfield, P.C. Haring, and Starla Huchton undertook this challenge. When it comes to podcasting fiction, the novel remains the Mount Everest of audio projects to undertake, with some authors never reaching the summit. Be it time, effort, or resources needed, final chapters remain unrecorded. Podcasting novels is not a casual undertaking by any means.

Together we have produced six podcast novels—or *podiobooks*, a term coined by Evo Terra in 2005. Terra later created Podiobooks.com, the premier location for podcast fiction. Some of our books were previously published, while others were released as audio before they saw print. In the process of podcasting six novels we learned a few valuable lessons.

- **DO NOT LAUNCH THE PODCAST NOVEL UNTIL IT IS COMPLETE.** In the early days, it was suggested that a *buffer* of episodes—perhaps five to ten—was good to have on hand. That way, if life happened to get in the way (and it usually would), you would still be able to keep a weekly or a biweekly delivery schedule. Now it is commonly recommended that before the first episode launches, the podcast should be completed in its entirety. Long-form podcasting is especially difficult when attempting to maintain a regular schedule while balancing real life, so consider having your novel recorded from beginning to end before going live.

- **KEEP PRODUCTION AT A MINIMUM.** While indulging in various aspects of production—sound effects, guest voices, and music— is fun in short-form podcasting, long-form podcasting offers demands of its own. Such production elements only slow your progress. Keep the production in your podcast novel simple. If you want to add more elements, do so, but remember that you are increasing your workload.
- **WITH A COMPLETE PODIOBOOK, ADHERE TO YOUR POSTING SCHEDULE.** A complete podiobook means you can set your posting schedule: weekly, biweekly, twice a week, etc. In doing so, you are making a commitment and have no legitimate reason to shirk off responsibility—so stick to your schedule.

BOOKMARK

Be careful what you wish for, or, in the case of podcasting, be careful when you ask for feedback. You're most likely to get it—and from places you may not expect. Since geography doesn't limit the distance your podcast can travel, unlike terrestrial radio, you may receive feedback from listeners coast to coast and around the world. And just like book reviews, feedback isn't guaranteed praise. Listeners will be *honest* with you. Respect that.

WHY SHOULD YOU PODCAST?

If it sounds like there is a lot of work involved in just planning and producing a podcast, it's because there is. There's no other way to put it. When an idea for a podcast comes to you, it is just like when an idea comes to you for a book. A lot of planning, effort, and resources go into a podcast, and when authors try to cut corners and run on the fly without a plan, the results can be disastrous.

Don't believe us? Search the variety of podcasts about writing on iTunes. You might notice that some *podfade* (a term for when a podcast starts strong, only to soon peter out) after a mere three episodes. When a podcast includes ten minutes of a writer typing, signing books at a bookstore (without any context, such as where he is, when it happened, or what book he was signing), or revealing the contents of a shoe closet, you can safely assume some planning was sorely needed but didn't occur.

Yes. A *shoe closet*. We've seen a lot of bad podcasts in our day, and the examples we give above are out there on iTunes to this day.

Podcasts can be far more work intensive than blogging, but there are definite advantages to hosting either a show or an anthology.

PODCASTING FICTION IS A GREAT WAY TO INTRODUCE YOURSELF AND YOUR WORK TO AUDIENCES. Whether you decide to share an anthology of your backlogged short stories or your novel in its entirety, podcasts offer a "try before you buy" for potential fans all around the world. An anthology also doubles as great promotion for upcoming works, particularly a series, as the stories take nothing away from the novel you have coming; instead, these short stories introduce listeners to the world and offer glimpses at the novel's principal players. For a podiobook novel, your podcast could be a prequel or separate story running in time with the events of your main novel, offering listeners a low-risk, free introduction to your world, style, and work.

PODCASTS OFFER AUDIENCES AN INTIMATE BEHIND-THE-SCENES LOOK AT BEING A WRITER. Many still believe the author's life to be all about ascots, smoking jackets, and enjoying snifters of cognac while the sun sets. If this is true, we have failed as professional authors.

Well, we do own ascots—we write steampunk—so that's covered.

Podcast talk shows not only dispel those lofty myths, they tear down the fourth wall between writer and reader, inviting the audience into the process. Sometimes authors express themselves with breakdowns of world building, character development, and plotting. Other times, the focus is not on work but on play: what they are currently reading, a live report from a conference or author event, or two authors talking about how they unwind. The podcast is your chance to sit down with your readers and allow them to get to know you beyond your pages.

PODCASTING, WHETHER IT IS FICTION OR A VARIETY SHOW, IS JUST PLAIN FUN. "All work and no play makes Jack [Torrance] a dull boy," so why not fire up the microphones and let loose? Some of the best podcasts we have recorded have been in the studio with other authors, either talking about what we do when planning and plotting, or what we do when we are off the clock. Podcasts can be very therapeutic that way, helping you manage stress, deadlines, writer's block, and a variety of other speed bumps that life can unexpectedly throw your way. You can also find joy in taking someone's audio fiction and enhancing it with music and sounds to bring it to life. And then there is the accomplishment of finishing your own podiobook, releasing it to the public, and hearing someone say, "I heard the podcast, so I really needed to read the book." Podcasting is a rewarding experience and, with the right plan and the right strategy, it can be as equally satisfying as the release date of your latest novel.

Podcasting sounded like a neat hobby. I had always liked the idea of being on the radio, but I get tongue-tied, and recording and editing myself was easier. I'm not sure if I had gone into it with the focus of building a career, I wouldn't have chickened out. But since I was just doing it for fun, I wasn't afraid of failing, so I "accidentally" built an audience of people who were eager to hear my work, both nonfiction and fiction. I wouldn't have the career I have today if I hadn't started podcasting in 2004. So the lesson I learned was: Don't be afraid of failing.

—MUR LAFFERTY, CAMPBELL AND PARSEC AWARD WINNER
AND AUTHOR OF GHOST TRAIN TO NEW ORLEANS

WHY SHOULDN'T YOU PODCAST?

This may sound like a real stunner coming from two podcast novelists, but after success—both creatively and critically—with podcasting, we will never be podcasting long-form fiction again.

Maybe right about now, you're thinking, "Woah-woah-woah! You two are longtime podcasters, and you've just spent a section of this book telling me how great it is to podcast. Now you're saying not?"

One more time—we will not be podcasting *long-form* fiction any time soon.

We love podcasting, and we love to podcast fiction, but there are a few reasons we've made this call. Podcasting is a blast, but it is not for everyone, and podcasting a novel means less time for our writing. Along with talk shows and anthologies, we believe it is only fair to talk about how podcasting can work against the author, just so you know what you are facing when considering one.

PODCASTING IS A FINANCIAL INVESTMENT: A podcast can't happen without a *microphone*, and if you want your show to have a clean, quality sound, a mic built into your computer won't cut it. In addition, you're going to need *recording software*. There are free options out there, but professional packages, such as Audition and Logic Pro X, offer more features, better mixing capabilities, and export formats. To handle any outside noise, you may also want to invest in sound-dampening tiles, or something similar. The more you invest in a podcast, the better your production will sound, but it all depends on your budget. How much do you want to invest in a production that will earn you nothing directly? If you are not ready to make the investment, then you probably should reconsider podcasting as a promotional avenue for yourself.

OVERSHARING: A podcast can be a challenge to produce, but without parameters or personal borders, it can become a therapist's couch if you're not careful. As mentioned before, podcasts provide an intimate connection between you and your readers, but unchecked, that intimacy can put you, your family, and your professional reputation at risk. Recording your thoughts or opinions after having a "bad day" at a book signing, with an editor, or at an agent meeting could descend into muckraking, and once a rant has gone live, it is distributed into the various media players of your subscribers, remaining there even when you remove it from your server. You should know, well before your first podcast, what you do and do not want to talk about.

RELYING ON CONTENT FROM OTHERS: Even with money exchanging hands, waiting for content from others can be a disappointment, especially if deadlines are missed. Without the agreed-upon content, the time you were hoping to save by having someone else provide the podcast will be lost. Additionally, if someone writes you a story, but refuses to record it, no time is saved on your end. When audio comes from somewhere other than your own studio, it may not have the quality you strive for, and while you can't necessarily expect studio-quality audio, you may need to work some post-production audio engineering. That means you need more time to replace the content.

PODCASTING IS AN INVESTMENT IN TIME: We did some math on the time we spent on our podcast novels. For the amount of time we poured into one of our long-form podcast fiction titles, we could have easily written two novels. To be fair, we love production elements, including guest voices. But all those audio dimensions add time to producing a single episode; even if you keep it simple by using just a bit of stock music for scene changes, you will still need to edit out breaks, stammers, and places where the speaker trips up. Editing audio also requires review. Cut off too much from an audio take and the timing between the beginning and end of the edit may sound unnatural. Additionally, missed edits or repeats may sneak into the episode. Podcasting long-form fiction, even when kept to the basics, demands time. Are you ready to make that investment?

WHY DO WE STILL PODCAST?

We're sure it sounds like we are sending you mixed messages on podcasting, but it's more of a "You need to know what you are getting yourselves into" situation. Authors love the idea of getting behind the microphone and riffing away, but once you get beyond the newness of it, podcasting can be a real undertaking.

That said, we love podcasting and still podcast to this day. When you podcast short fiction—original episodes set within the world of your novel—these audio adventures can broaden the universe you're creating and enhance the reader's experience, provided you set a strategy. With the first season of our *Tales from the Archives* podcast, we introduced potential readers to our cog-and-gear-enhanced world through lost cases of the Ministry of Peculiar Occurrences. These adventures predated events of our premier novel, *Phoenix Rising*. Initially we planned for the podcast to be a glimpse into what we had created. However, when readers began asking if our audio anthology would reveal more of Wellington Books's past, the Ministry embarking on adventures in other parts of Her Majesty's empire, and whether or not there were other agencies similar to the Ministry investigating the unknown in other places in the world, we needed to change our strategy.

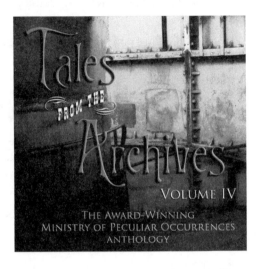

Three of the stories from that first season—"The Evil That Befell Samson" by Pip Ballantine, "The Seven" by P.C. Haring, and "From Paris, With Regret" by Starla Huchton—went one step further and referenced events mentioned in *Phoenix Rising*. This, we discovered, was a real treat for readers as they felt the podcast offered an added dimension to the novel. Now, several Parsec Awards (an award bestowed to the best in speculative fiction podcasting), four seasons, and a "change of strategy" later, select characters, situations, and even artifacts from the podcast are making appearances in the novels, and vice versa. Some stories even carry an impact on future novels. These references (commonly known as *Easter eggs*) from the podcast expand a book's reach, granting you and your readers plenty of new avenues to explore. What was once a marketing tool, the *Tales from the Archives* podcast now provides a "Director's Cut" approach to the series, offering additional scenes audiences delight in experiencing.

As for our talk show, *The Shared Desk*, we employ a different strategy. There are other goals of promotion—letting people know where we will be and what our upcoming projects are, and sharing writing topics that interest us—but in the end, the aim of *The Shared Desk* is to unwind a bit. We do, and we manage events of interest to the writer while doing so. We now have the podcast down to a system that allows us to record with little-to-no post-production (although we do sometimes come across a few things that should remain unsaid and therefore must be edited out), so all that we need is a topic and a chunk of time.

Author, photographer, and artist J.R. Blackwell says *The Shared Desk* is "just like having a drink with Tee & Pip ..." and we take a lot of pride in that. We enjoy that connection with our readers, fans, and friends, but with deadlines, demands of family, and (of course) writing, there are occasional "silent spells" that one of our more passionate listeners, Gail Carriger, has chastised Tee for.

And when you upset Gail Carriger, you can rest assured when having tea—*no scones for you, mate.*

Podcasts can be all about promotion, but they should also be fun. With the amount of effort and planning that go into them, they should always be fun. This is what drives us to keep going.

The Shared Desk, with the publication of this book, will be offering a special "social media-centric" episode once a month (the show posts on a biweekly schedule) on the OneStopWriterShop.com blog. If you want to subscribe to only the audio addendums for this book, subscribe to the One-Stop Writer Shop blog. If you want all the shenanigans that go on behind the mic, subscribe to *The Shared Desk* through iTunes or TheSharedDesk.com.

Podcasting can be quite an intimate, personal experience. But now we're going to dive right into the largest social media platform currently out there. Hold onto your headphones and warm up your Liking finger as we head into the wild open spaces of Mark Zuckerberg's world.

The King of Social Media

If social media began with blogging, then Facebook is what it has transformed into today. Running for just over a decade, and sporting a membership of over 1 billion users, Facebook is the force of nature in social media that people hate to love and love to hate.

But what is it that makes Facebook so appealing?

Before Facebook, social networking covered a wide variety of websites and applications. If you wanted to express an opinion and invite an audience to comment on your thoughts, you would blog. If you had photos you wanted to share, you would upload your photos to Flickr and share links or embed your images in blog posts. If you wanted to swap a quick note with friends, you would use either AOL Instant Messenger, Yahoo! Messenger, or Skype. This meant hopping across multiple locations to share media, touch base, and keep people in the know.

That all changed when Facebook brought to the Internet a one-stop website where photos could be uploaded and shared, thoughts in both long and short form could be posted, comments on these thoughts could be responded to with links, images, or both, and private messages could be shared with others online. With everything offered in one location, it's easy to see how Facebook erupted in popularity and became the "necessary evil" in building your social media platform.

We will address the description of "necessary evil" for Facebook later in this chapter. Right now, let's take a closer look at Facebook and what it can do for writers.

FACEBOOK FOR WRITERS

Signing up on Facebook is only the first step. Perhaps the most important question of this social network is that of your intent. Do you want Facebook to be a means to communicate with friends and family? Or do you want to run Facebook as a professional platform?

What's the difference? An audience of about five hundred as opposed to five thousand.

Chances are, without professional acquaintances, your Facebook friends would not extend beyond a few hundred, but as a writer using Facebook as a promotional platform, you may be approving friendships with people you know only from a meeting at a conference or the purchase of a book. This is where the line blurs between personal and professional relationships in social media. Along with various strategies on how to leverage Facebook in your favor, we will talk about this line and how best to define it.

You have to stay flexible, because you don't know where the "next big thing" is coming from. Right now, Facebook is ubiquitous. I get more interaction from Facebook than any other platform. It's easy to keep readers informed and easy for them to reach out to the author via comments on text and image posts. As Facebook ramps up video, I think it will create a great opportunity for authors to make fast, simple videos that help readers identify with the person behind the words.

—SCOTT SIGLER, *NEW YORK TIMES* BEST-SELLING AUTHOR OF *ALIVE*

Facebook grants you two ways to work with an audience and, outside of your main account, keep a separation between the personal life and professional one: *Groups* and *Pages*. Groups are a community built around a shared interest, while Pages are more of a central hub of information where a host controls the signal, frequency, and variety of content.

Where Everybody Knows Your Name: Groups

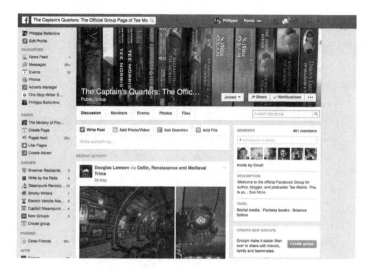

First, let's take a look at *Groups*. Groups are communities built around a cause or commonalities like electric vehicle owners, cancer survivors, a reoccurring special event, or fans of science fiction and fantasy. The online club is a great way to encourage and build an active, enthusiastic community around your work and your worlds, as the content featured on Groups is completely community driven. Everyone shares a voice here, but since the discussion only happens when someone speaks up, it's a good idea to have a few topics ready for discussion before you invite readers and other authors to join. Having topics on hand also helps you avoid lulls in the Group's activity.

The most recent post made by a member will appear at the top of your Group. This is the case until someone leaves a comment, restoring that topic to the top of the feed. Interaction takes priority with all previous topics until a new topic is posted.

Along with general discussions, you can upload photos and videos, ask questions of your Group members with a poll, or add a file (PDF, Word document, etc.) to share with your membership. Provided the media falls under the guidelines of your group, this is a great way to share exclusive content with your community.

BOOKMARK

If you are a *Moderator*, or someone else in your Group is assigned as Moderator, you are Judge Dredd: judge, jury, and executioner. If you make your Group *public*, you decide who stays and who goes on account of bad behavior. With *private* groups, you also decide who is invited. Moderators must not only keep an eye on the behavior of members and the approval of new ones, but they must also make certain members stay on topic. Gone unchecked, Groups can become havens for trolls (people who are deliberately provocative, just to get a reaction) and spambots. Moderation is paramount, just as it is for a blog, to keep your signal strong and the conversation of a high quality. Set ground rules for your Group, and adhere to them. Otherwise, a community can quickly fall apart.

Groups are fantastic for creating a community, but if you are promoting a new release or even a short story in an upcoming anthology and someone in the community posts about seeing your book in a bookstore or promoting his own project, then your own post concerning your latest release may be lost. With enough interaction, you can manage to keep your post at the top of a Group's feed, but only until someone leaves a comment on a previous post, once again burying your promotion under previous posts.

Instead of using Groups as a place to promote yourself and your works, use it to create a community around a cause, an event, or a passion. Perhaps you want to host a writer's group—a safe place (provided you enforce your own guidelines) for writers of all skill levels and backgrounds to refine their storytelling talents. You would not use the same strategy you used to implement a *Page* (more on that to come), but it would be a fantastic way to get your name out there in a spirit of goodwill. The focus with a Group like this should not be all on you, but you can easily claim your Group and its intent, a very subtle strategy of self-promotion if it becomes popular.

So if this is a Group, what is a Page?

My House, My Rules: Pages

While a Group is a community that shares something in common and meets in one location to discuss it openly, a *Page* is very different in two respects. First, Pages come with an *administrator's control panel* (or *admin panel*) that features built-in *analytics* (measurements of traffic coming to and from your Page, demographics, and performance of ad campaigns), options for boosting posts (paid advertisements), and options to schedule posts (you can either post immediately or schedule a time for your message to appear in Facebook's *News Feed*). Another difference between Pages and Groups is that moderators for Pages post as the host, whether that's as a business, a celebrity, or an organization. People who Like a Page can interact with page updates, but they cannot post updates unless they are admins. These posts appear in the News Feed, regardless of whether you are following that page or not.

People on Facebook know more about Pages than Groups simply because of the language and open promotion in the world outside of the Internet. (Yes, there is this magical place called "Outside," and it is where this thing called "Life" happens.) You rarely hear individuals, businesses, or people at events say "Join our Group on Facebook." Instead, audiences, patrons, and fans of various venues—restaurants, historical sites, and parks—are told "Like Us on Facebook" which remains the best, most efficient way to stay in the know.

When creating a Facebook Page you want to make certain your Page is complete. Remember that just as with a blog and a podcast, a Facebook Page should have all its information complete in order to make the best first impression that you can.

Your Page's Profile Picture

While you have the option to rotate images in and out of visibility, this representation of you and your work should rarely change. If you are an author, this should be your current head shot or a custom logo designed for you and your books. If you create a Page for a series, it should be the most current cover or, as stated earlier, a custom logo that belongs to you. This is your *brand*, and when people glance at it they should be able to easily connect this image with you or your business.

Your Cover Photo

Unlike a Profile Picture, your *Cover Photo* should be rotated for variety. The cover photo can display a number of things:

- Upcoming Events
- New Releases
- Upcoming Releases

You should find an image that serves as a "default" image (pertaining to your brand), but take advantage of the Cover Photo as one of the promotion tools in your arsenal.

The Like Option

When accessing your Page, you can see whether you have Liked this Page or not. It's not vain to Like your own Page, as this is a way to monitor your own feed. Anything you share or post will appear on your personal feed, assuring you that the Page's posts are getting out.

BOOKMARK

Since February 2014, Facebook has been changing its algorithms to make *organic reach* (growth and signal coverage through people sharing your posts) much harder to cultivate on Pages. Now, for subscribers to your Page, there is no guarantee your posts will be seen without *boosting* (paid promotion) posts.

Something you can do to increase the chances of your posts being seen is to tell Facebook you wish to *Get Notifications* from a page you've liked. Move your cursor over the Liked icon and select from the drop-down menu that appears the Get Notifications and Following options. You will then receive alerts whenever posts go live on the page.

The About Section

Here is where you provide the details and contact information for your business and online connections. To edit this information, click anywhere in the About section and click the Edit button to set up and edit Preferences, shared information, and Administrator roles. This is where you provide links to your main site and your bibliography, and details about you or your works.

The Post Section

From this section of the Facebook Page, administrators can post status updates, links, announcements, photos and videos, and special events and milestones. These are the announcements that will appear on the *Updates Feed* of the Page.

Making a post on a Page is similar to making a post with a Group, with the exception of two points. First, your post—if you are an Administrator—will appear with the name of the Page, not *your* name, unless you select an option other than the Page's name from a drop-down menu. (This posting option is available in the Comments section as well.) The other difference with posting on a Page is that updates will appear in the Page's Updates Feed in the order of posting, from the most recent at the top to older posts as you progress down the Page.

Earning Likes from Your Fans

Your Page is up and running. Congratulations! Now's the time to go hunting for the ever-elusive Likes.

Why do we use "ever-elusive" to describe earning Likes? According to TechCrunch, as of April 29, 2015, more than forty million Pages are active. Forty *million*. You might think "Why bother?" but then Facebook reports that out of the forty million Pages, only two million are active.

What does *that* mean?

For some businesses and organizations, Pages are built and then abandoned after giving social media a try. How that "try" is defined is nebulous. These active two million are not reliant on organic reach and viral content alone. They are building a presence, a personality, and a reputation on Facebook. Social media is not simply throwing a switch and welcoming adoring fans to your corner of a network. Time and strategy achieve success on Facebook.

So out of those two million active Pages, how do you get readers to Like your Page, provided they can find it?

"Go Like My Page" Posts

Probably the most common way to get your numbers up is by asking for Likes. Subtle ways of doing this include the use of print materials (business cards, postcards, etc.) that say to "Like Us on Facebook." Restaurants, movies, bands, and all kinds of businesses employ this simple method. The more direct method is to compose a post that asks people to swing by your Page and Like it. Asking directly for Likes is not considered bad form, provided this approach does not dominate your feed. Repeated requests degrade the quality of your Page from signal to noise, and eventually from noise to spam.

A once-a-week reminder, provided there is a variety of content in your feed, can serve as a polite, proactive approach to increasing your numbers.

Embedding Page Links

A more subtle way of promoting your Page is to link back to it through other posts. Provided you have Liked a Page, linking back to a Page is easy.

When you click Share to circulate a Facebook post on another Page, your personal feed, or a friend's feed, a new window appears that displays the original post and a link back to the Facebook Page of origin, offering people a direct connection back to you.

Another way to embed a link into a post (whether the post is shared or original) is to begin typing a Page you have Liked in the

Post field. You begin with the @ symbol and then type the name of the Page you wish to link to. A drop-down menu appears, offering options for pages that share similar titles. Continue typing the Page's name until your option appears. After selecting your desired Page, a highlighted link will appear in the post.

BOOKMARK

If you have Liked other Pages, sometimes you are offered options of names, places, and businesses that match up with what you are typing, even without adding the @ symbol to typed message.

Your post is now live, sporting two ways for people to find your Page. This is a subtle, elegant way of promoting your work while sharing quality content.

Print Materials

When attending book events, you will see banners, flyers, postcards, and even business cards, all featuring an author's website, e-mail, and maybe even a Twitter account in lieu of a phone number. If you can find a place to promote your Page, either on the back cover or in the interior front matter of your books, make it happen. If you're going to promote a Facebook Page in print, it is paramount to have a URL that's easy for people to remember and easy to read in print, like facebook.com/TheMinistryOfPeculiarOccurrences or facebook.com/onestopwriter, both of which neatly fit on a business card.

Boosting Posts and Pages

As we mentioned earlier in this chapter, Facebook periodically changes its algorithms for News Feeds so that previously Liked pages no longer appeared automatically in your feed. The official word from Facebook was "We're getting to a place where because more people are sharing more things, the best way to get your stuff seen if you're a business is to pay for it."[1] Across blogs like Mashable[2] and BusinessesGrow,[3] Pages have reported major hits on their Organic Reach for businesses, particularly for medium, small, and (in the case of authors) sole proprietor businesses. We personally know of some cases where organic reach plummeted by 90 percent.

In order to boost a Post or Page, you have to pay Facebook a fee. In turn, it promotes the signal of a single post or the entire Page. Doing so can make a huge difference in your reach, at least according to the analytics. But are people actually seeing your advertisements or simply scrolling past them in order to get to that cute kitten picture? Between boosting individual posts or Pages, we have found that boosting individual posts is a smarter tactic. Not every post, mind you, as that would smell a bit of spam. (And let's be honest, you don't want your page to reek of the scent of *spam*.) Promoted posts should cover key topics worth your money:

- new book releases
- exclusive events
- award announcements

It is up to you to decide if boosting a post is worth the financial investment, but be smart about where your money goes with Facebook. Most writers have a limited budget and therefore must be careful about where they invest. *Think* about where you really want to direct your readers' eyeballs.

BOOKMARK

The video blog Veritasium is well known for featuring experiments, sharing interviews with leading minds of science, and showing demonstrations of chemistry and physics that will make you go "Woah!" But on February 10, 2014, its host Derek Muller released a fascinating study[4] on how Facebook

---

1 http://adage.com/article/digital/facebook-admits-organic-reach-brand-posts-dipping/245530/

2 http://mashable.com/2013/12/30/marketers-facebook-rules/

3 http://www.businessesgrow.com/2014/01/29/paying-for-reach/

4 http://bit.ly/fb-fraud

handles Likes that users purchase. Accumulating a staggering three million views (and still climbing), Muller goes deep into the slightly unethical business Facebook has started where "engagement" is the last thing Page hosts can expect. This video is a worthwhile watch when you're debating whether or not purchasing Likes for your Page is the right move.

CONTENT MARKETING: THE SCIENCE OF PROMOTION BY EXAMPLE

Logic would tell you that investing in paid reach should be the easiest way to get the word out about you and your books. It would be logical, but in truth, you are more likely to win the lottery than to find a post that resonates across the board with *everyone* online. Yes, having wildfire appeal similar to *The Fault in Our Stars* or *The Hunger Games* would be a beautiful thing to happen to your book, and you know better than anyone that your work has that potential, but trying to reach everyone through paid promotion on a limited budget is unrealistic.

Visit our Ministry of Peculiar Occurrences Page for a great example of how odd the search for viral content can be. You'll find a cross section of various posts we have boosted and others we have posted because we thought were really cool steampunk topics to post. You can see the dramatic difference between the traffic of all the posts, and how even "throwing money" at the posts did not necessarily equate reach or engagement compared to the posts that received no boost at all. The truth of Facebook is that there's no magic bullet, no sure-fire formula, and no foolproof way to gain traction. Sometimes it will be the post about your book that will garner you traffic and numbers; other times an eye-catching post from the Internet will boost your numbers.

That's why *content marketing* is the cost-effective trend worth practicing. It's a promotional approach based not on the repetition of advertising, but on the reputation and quality of a subject matter.

What matters in content marketing is *quality*, not quantity, of your Page's posts. If you provide your Page followers with good material, turning your Page into a go-to source for reliable resources and fantastic media, you establish a connection with your audience. When people are searching on Facebook for that page with the best content on a subject—news from the romance genre, the latest releases in science fiction, or what's happening in the steampunk community—you want them to instantly think of you. That recognition, based on the reputation you are building through consistent and relevant content you are posting, will lead people to your Page. An additional boon to content marketing is the rapport you build with others in your business. As people find your work through content related to it, sharing websites, blog posts, and other media from your peers, you build a reputation with readers, book bloggers, and authors. You let them know that you are not just a writer, but also a passionate, encouraging supporter of your genre and the writing community as a whole.

When Content Marketing Goes Bad

Content marketing can be a positive, community-building strategy for any individual or business, whether you're a writer, a publisher, or even a literary agency. However, some writers and social media mavericks regard the features of Facebook to be up for grabs and turn your content into instant viral content. One unethical approach to sharing content on Facebook takes advantage of the *photo tagging* feature.

If you are unfamiliar with photo tagging, this feature is engaged when you upload a photograph or video to Facebook. You are given an option at the bottom of the photo to Tag Photo. With this option, you can identify someone in the photo, a live link is created to your account, and then the image appears on your Timeline.

Unethical authors—and, yes, this has happened to us on numerous occasions—will grab a photograph promoting their book, be it subtle or straight up in your face, and then tag you in the picture. Suddenly a random picture that has nothing to do with an event you attended or anything remotely related to you appears on your Timeline, openly promoting another author's book. You have the option of removing your tag from any innocuous images, but remember that some authors will exercise the right to tag you in the image *again*.

Yes, this also has happened to us.

If you are tagging other authors in photos, be sure that they depict something relevant. By relevant, we mean an appearance at which the author is seen in the picture, the cover of an anthology where their work appears, or something that you know will appeal to their tastes. (Tee has lost count of the number of times the "steampunk barbecue grill" has appeared on his Timeline, but he doesn't mind. He loves both a good barbecue and good steampunk. That picture is the best of both.) Tagging photos to specifically promote yourself is nothing less than spam.

Another dark side of content marketing is establishing a Page with only one goal: collecting thousands upon thousands of Likes in order to eventually sell the Page to the highest bidder. Ways that some of these *Like Farms* (as mentioned in the earlier Veritasium Bookmark) collect massive numbers include:

- Meme Generation
- Quizzes
- Content Scraping

In Chapters 12 and 13, which cover content marketing and best practices in depth, we will discuss conventions that are considered questionable or unethical, what to avoid not only on Facebook but also on all social media platforms, and how to best avoid these pitfalls.

Facebook is attempting to crack down on these unethical approaches, but keeping tabs on over a billion users is a daunting task. When putting together your own Page, a good question to ask yourself is "What am I going to do with all these Likes on my Page?" While it is easy to lose yourself in the numbers game of social media, quality should always trump quantity. Aim not only to cultivate a strong support system on your Page, but also for essential, relevant content that will bring people to your Page and keep them coming back.

Sometimes Facebook can be very confusing when trying to find your readers among your friends, your family, and all these other folks with accounts, Groups, and Pages. We hope that in this chapter you have discovered some ways to clear the undergrowth from the depths of the forest of Facebook and perhaps learned how to best spend your marketing budget along the way.

Next, you'll take things down a notch and learn how to communicate with readers in 140 characters. There is a myth that you can't say a lot within such limitations, that all you can do is promote your book by title and links, share what others are talking about, or post quick and pithy quotes from famous people. In reality, the 140 characters Twitter affords can provide a teaser for upcoming books, connect you with other fans, and help you do research for—or even inspire—your next novel.

CHAPTER 5

Twitter

Keeping It Brief

When it comes to a user-friendly interface and a true plug-and-play spirit, it rarely comes as easy as Twitter. The service has gone through different stages of use, popularity, and application. In its early days, Twitter was a terrific tool to stay in touch and communicate with friends. But just a few years later, it became rife with self-appointed social media gurus who pass along inspirational quotes, needless spam of all varieties, and tweets from other accounts. Unfortunately, that's the price of popularity.

Twitter still serves as a reliable, trusted mobile communication option and is regarded as one of the cornerstones in setting up a strong social media platform. It also now acts as an extension of other popular networks like LinkedIn, Pinterest, and Instagram. Twitter is many different things to many people, and it serves various purposes for writers:

- A connection with other authors, both for professional networking and for finding new and unique resources for their work
- A promotional platform for works currently in print or digital formats, and for special offers concerning their works
- A direct line of communication to fans, making their day with a quick reply

It's hard not to have a love/hate relationship with Twitter. Hate because it can be a time suck and can often make us crazy. But there's so much to love for those in publishing and for writers in particular: an opportunity to move outside our introverted selves and have direct conversations with the readers who love our books, the ability to interact with people who have the same love of the written word we do, and more than anything, the chance to discover our next great read. Twitter brings us together to celebrate books and that's worth loving!

—ANGELA JAMES, EDITORIAL DIRECTOR OF HARLEQUIN'S CARINA PRESS AND CREATOR OF THE POPULAR BEFORE YOU HIT SEND, A SELF-EDITING WORKSHOP FOR FICTION WRITERS

Twitter is easy to get right, but it can be a nightmare for you and your followers if you get it wrong.

FIRST IMPRESSIONS AT A GLANCE

When people arrive on your Twitter profile page, what do they see? Do you have a profile picture that introduces you to potential followers? Does this profile picture represent how you want to be perceived? How about the header photo stretching across the top of the page? Is there something there that completes your profile page? What does your bio say about you? Is it complete? Is it snarky? All these details are part of the first impression that you and your Twitter account make.

An Author's Profile Photo: Worth a Thousand Tweets

Approach a profile picture the same way you would an appearance at a bookstore, a conference, or a writing festival. The author who shows up to a panel discussion prepared for the topic at hand, presenting himself in a professional manner, will be regarded differently than the writer who has not bothered to prepare for the topic and looks as if she couldn't bother to brush her hair or find a better shirt to wear than an "I Love Books" T-shirt. The photo you assign to your Twitter account becomes your *personal brand*, representing who you are and what you do.

For profile pictures, images should be:

- File size: 700 KB
- Dimensions: 400 × 400 pixels (Twitter offers you cropping options, but this is the recommended size.)

- Resolution: 72 ppi (pixels per inch)
- Format: JPEG or PNG file, using the RGB color scale

Before you start tweeting, your priority is to get away from Twitter's default image (an egg) and find a profile picture that best represents you. Does your current picture, or the one you're considering, make the professional impression you desire? Does your brand have a sense of humor, or is it more polished? Camera phones and simple photo editors make profile pictures a breeze, but what should you use and what should you avoid? What are your options?

Option One: A Picture of You

Perhaps the simplest and best way to introduce yourself to people is with a pesonal photo that puts a face to the Twitter handle—a personal connection. Depending on your creativity, you can use this kind of profile picture to reflect your particular mood. Perhaps you're going to a special event and you snap a selfie on the way out the door. Maybe you have new haircut you're proud of. Perhaps a picture of you and your pet might cheer someone up on a Monday morning. You really never know what will strike the interest of your readers, but showing them a peek behind the curtain is a good way to start.

Before you use your smartphone of choice to take a quick selfie or run out to find that wicked-awesome photo of you in a tuxedo or evening dress, consider this approach:

- **USE PICTURES TAKEN FROM THE CHEST OR NECK UP:** Remember that those using Twitter applications, especially people on smartphones, will be looking at profile pictures dramatically reduced in dimension. Full-body shots of you will be imperceptible. Keep your photo tightly cropped and close up.
- **AVOID IMAGES WITH BUSY BACKGROUNDS:** What is happening behind you is just as important as how you look. Too much detail or activity in the background (what some photographers refer to as "noise") can make profile pictures on Twitter difficult to make out. Keep what's happening behind you to the basics.

- **AVOID OFFENSIVE IMAGERY:** This could prove a challenge for horror and erotica authors, because what is deemed "offensive" differs from person to person. Use your best judgment. No nudity. Refrain from obscene gestures. Keep the gore level to the bare minimum.

Option Two: A Personal Logo

Branding was associated in the past with business, public relations, and marketing strategies. Today, with modern authors shouldering the promotion of their books, this concept is no longer reserved for advertising agencies to pitch to corporate entities and charge top dollar. Authors are taking to heart principles of branding and applying them to their networking outlets, like Twitter.

A simplified definition of branding is an approach to your business through association with a word, catchphrase, or image. You see it everywhere. Two golden arches usually mean a McDonald's is within sight. A stylized arrowhead worn just over the left breast might make you think of *Star Trek*. A bird against a certain shade of blue taking flight? That's Twitter. If you have a product or a service that people associate with a phrase, name, or some other identifier, then you have successful, effective branding.

Creating a brand offers a unique set of challenges:

- **MAKE SURE YOUR LOGO IS ORIGINAL, AND YOUR OWN.** You might think this is common sense, but individuals may be tempted to parody corporate giants or make a variation on another's theme. Don't do it. It's best to come up with something original. Make it your own. Make it unique.
- **AVOID TEXT-HEAVY OR BUSY IMAGES AS PERSONAL LOGOS.** Keep it simple. If your self-designed or professionally commissioned logo comes with tag lines, pen names, or URLs, accept that such things will be lost when rendered smaller than 75 × 75 pixels. For our multimedia studio, Imagine That!, our brand is a stylized double koru—the fern frond that is a symbol of new life and growth. For One-Stop Writer Shop, the logo is a stop sign with a

book at its center. Remember: The busier you make it, the harder it will be to recognize it at a glance. Logo designs are best when basic.

- **BRANDING DOES NOT HAPPEN OVERNIGHT.** Use your logo beyond Twitter and give yourself time for brand recognition. When we release our books or book trailers under the Imagine That! banner, we make sure the logo is visible. Any materials produced from One-Stop Writer Shop bear the stop sign logo. Use your logo consistently and constantly in your promotional materials and you will build brand recognition for yourself.

Option Three: Interests, Hobbies, or Something Out of the Ordinary

For the I-really-hate-to-be-photographed or the I-really-have-zero-artistic-ability authors, there is another option. From zombified George Washington to a variety of characters from video games (any from the eight-bit days to modern *Halo* resolutions) to celebrities of various backgrounds, profile pictures that are not about you, but about your interests, may be used. However, ask yourself what these images do for you in the way of branding. The answer is absolutely nothing. Do they make a connection with your network? If individuals in your network are into whatever your profile picture depicts, sure, provided you continue to talk about that particular interest. The people following your network may not even know about your writing career unless you mention it in your profile.

If, however, you would rather keep a distance between your network and your own likeness—and it's not uncommon for authors to want to do so—then this option will work well for you. It maintains a sense of privacy for the concerned author and can even serve as a mood indicator, as this option does not commit you to one particular profile picture. When you use a picture of Animal in full rave out, a photo of Furiosa behind the wheel of her war rig, or Captain Kirk screaming into his communicator, people will know you're having a bad day.

The problem with swapping out avatars is the loss of brand recognition. As mentioned earlier, branding works only when an image is used repeatedly so that eventually consumers associate you or your company with it. If you want to take advantage of that recognition, keep your profile picture consistent.

Of course, there are exceptions to this rule, and there are ways to continue branding while swapping out profile pictures. During the Christmas holidays, we usually post images of us wearing stocking caps. Be smart about how you swap out profile pictures. Decide on a strategy and try to find consistency with the image you are portraying.

Now that you have a profile photo in place, let's take a closer look at the header photo for your profile page.

The Header Photo: Setting a Tone on Twitter

Twitter has been refining its profile pages since the introduction of the header photo back in 2012. Similar to the Facebook cover photo, which also incorporates a banner-style photo option on both personal profiles and Pages, the header photo is a space where you can add a favorite horizontal photo as set dressing for your profile. If the profile photo is your first impression, the header photo is your stage, offering either an atmosphere or a tone for your Twitter account. Is your Twitter account going to be full of whimsy, or controversial? This can be inferred from your profile picture. Think of how an author head shot on the back of a book can give you a feeling of what is inside.

Header photos are much like their Profile counterparts with a few differences here and there:

- File size: 5 MB (maximum)
- Dimensions: 1500 × 1500 pixels (Twitter offers you cropping and positioning options. This is the recommended size.)
- Resolution: 72 ppi (pixels per inch)
- Format: JPEG or PNG file, using RGB color scale

Something like the header photo may seem like a trivial detail, but it can bring a lot of pizzazz to your Twitter profile. Header photos can also change when you feel change is needed. It's at the author's discretion.

- **MAKE SURE HEADER PHOTOS ARE IN LANDSCAPE FORMAT.** In the case of Twitter's header photo, you need to think horizontally instead of vertically. Panoramic shots work best.
- **BE AS CREATIVE AND AS EXPRESSIVE AS YOU WILL.** The profile photo is how people identify you, but the header photo can be about you, your interests, and your passions. As a writer, this photo can showcase your favorite place to write, a stock photo of a library, or a (horizontal) portion of your book cover. You're setting a mood for your Twitter profile, so have some fun.
- **DESIGN HEADER PHOTOS USING THE RULE OF THIRDS.** Some header photos on Twitter appear jagged, out of focus, or distorted. This is Twitter's attempt to fill the header region with an image that's the wrong size or shape. Experiment with image sizes or design the image using horizontal thirds on a 1500 × 1500 canvas. You can check out the rule of thirds page on Wikipedia for a detailed explanation and design tips.[1]

Take into account how the header photo will appear on both the computer screen and the mobile app. Templates are available online to help you put the important part of the image in the part of the screen that will be friendly for both computer and mobile users.

---

1 http://en.wikipedia.org/wiki/Rule_of_thirds

What goes into a header photo is strictly up to you. As an author, it is not a bad idea to change your header photo to include a portion of your latest cover release, provided that the cover isn't too busy. For the more ambitious author who possesses a mastery of Adobe Photoshop, designing a banner to promote an upcoming event or release is a good idea. Unlike the profile photo, the header photo gives you a chance to express yourself, so use it to send a message. People will see this backdrop when they follow notifications directly to your profile, check out details on their smartphone, or visit other Twitter clients such as TweetDeck, a dashboard application used to manage Twitter accounts.

Now that we have a look for the profile, let's perfect that final touch.

Making an Introduction: The Twitter Bio

It's astounding how many authors leave this blank, or simply use it as yet another place to slap a link to their books. The bio, even within the limitations of 160 characters, is your opportunity to introduce yourself, and as an author, you want to make the best first impression you can. The bio is part of that.

Much like with profile and header photos, authors employ several ways of introducing themselves in their bios.

- **THE PROFESSIONAL APPROACH:**

  New York Times best-selling author of the INFECTED trilogy, NOC-TURNAL, ANCESTOR, the GFL series and upcoming ALIVE trilogy from Del Rey. Books!

  Scott Sigler, @scottsigler

  Campbell award-winning author Mur Lafferty. Podcaster. Ghost Train to New Orleans out now!

  Mur Lafferty, @mightymur

- **THE SNARKY APPROACH:**

  Reeling and Writhing

  Harper Voyager author Mary Victoria, @MAdamsVictoria

  I enjoy pie.

  Hugo-winning author John Scalzi, @scalzi

If you're going to go the snarky route, then we recommend you tread carefully. The above examples can't be taken in the wrong way. Keep it light and as amusing as possible.

- **SOMEWHERE IN BETWEEN:**

  Author of paranormal and sci-fi romance, steampunk and urban fantasy. Instigator of saucy hijinx and shenanigans.

  PJ Schnyder, @pjschnyder

  Kiwi word herder, cat wrangler, and collaborating creative. Somewhat responsible for Books of the Order, Shifted World, and Ministry of Peculiar Occurrences.

  Philippa Ballantine, @philippajane

WRITE A BIO THAT IS NOT OVERLOADED WITH LINKS. Some authors use their bios as a way to get in Google+ links, Facebook links, and others, but you don't want to do that. Instead write a bio that means something. Leave the URL for the URL field underneath the bio and location field.

AS WITH THE HEADER PHOTO, BE AS CREATIVE AS YOU LIKE. You can express your love of pie, use a quote that motivates you to write, or share your excitement about a debut novel coming soon to bookstores or e-readers. Your bio should be a sincere, succinct summary of what you are all about.

MAKE YOUR LOCATION AS CLOSE AS YOU WANT. Let people know where you are in the world. It can be as simple as the largest city closest to you, or which coast you are on. If you prefer, you can make your current location a state of mind.

HAVE YOUR URL GO TO YOUR MAIN SITE OR BLOG. One social media strategy we want you to get from this guide is the goal of sending traffic from social networks to your website. The final destination of your network should *not* be a platform like Twitter or Facebook. The destination should be your website, the corner of the Internet that has everything a reader needs to know about you, your works, and where you will be appearing next.

Following this profile audit, your first impression should be polished and ready for welcoming and connecting with new readers, fans of your works, and other authors. But what do you say? Is anyone really listening? And how do you say anything intelligent with only 140 characters?

It's time to embrace your inner editor and get over the fear of brevity. As Shakespeare once said, "Brevity is the soul of wit."

MASTERING TWEET SPEAK: COMPOSING MESSAGES ON TWITTER

All communication on Twitter begins with the statement you type into the message field, or what Twitter refers to as a *tweet*. When first introduced to Twitter, beginners often furrow their brow or roll their eyes at the cutesy name used for Twitter's updates.

Yes, an update on Twitter is called a "tweet." You're using an application on Twitter. Accept it, and move on.

The biggest pushback from authors continues to be the 140-characters-or-less limitation. You can't say a lot with that, right?

Actually, there is a lot you can say on Twitter. You just have to be smart and strategic about what you say, how you say it, and how you edit a detailed, in-depth post down to the essentials. Twitter requires an ability to understand and master an economy of words. You cannot necessarily speak your mind with the usual verbosity, which may surprise some users, but you can, *and must*, boil down what you *want* to say to what you *need* to say.

Let's say you want your first tweet to be the following:

> I'm awake this morning and waiting for the coffee to brew. I've got a big day ahead of me with edits, rewrites, and proposals all screaming for my attention. Oh yeah, and I've got an audiobook to get together for Audible. Yes, it looks a little overwhelming, but I'm feeling confident and ready to rock!

There are 304 characters (and that includes spaces) in this statement. While you could use apps that post tweets longer than 140-characters, most of these third-party services take people out of Twitter and to another website. Tweenjoy.com, for example, allows you write text beyond 140 characters, attaches an image with the text, and can even put in a header image as well. Another third-party app, Twinormous, breaks down your larger text into multiple tweets, which it will notate as one part of many parts. This might seem like a good idea, but if you have a lot of followers, your tweets might get separated in the stream and lose their context. Twitter users want to stay in Twitter, not hop over to another website to read a single tweet. They are also looking for a quick tweet where they can get what they need in that moment and then move on.

So presuming you're not going to go down either of those paths, let's break down the content of what you want to say. The main points of this 304-character tweet are:

- You're awake.
- The coffee is brewing.
- Your to-do list is very full for the day:

  - edits
  - rewrites
  - proposals
  - an audiobook for Audible

- You're feeling overwhelmed.
- Your confidence level is high, and you're ready to accomplish all these things!

All this needs to be one tweet. Take a look at this:

> Coffee brews as edits, rewrites, and proposals await. Kicking off the day with an @ACX_com submission. Let's make it happen. #determined

The original status of more than three hundred characters has been pruned down to 136 characters after making logical edits.

- You're tweeting, so no need to let us know you're awake.
- It's also clear you have a big day ahead as you have "edits, rewrites, and proposals" needing attention. So brew coffee while your projects wait for your attention.
- If you want to highlight the Audible project, tell your network you're "Kicking off the day with an @ACX_com submission." Mentioning Audible by using its handle can attract its attention and maybe even start up an exchange or earn you a retweet.
- If you're feeling confident and ready to rock, sum it up in one affirmation: "Let's make it happen."
- At this point you have fourteen characters remaining. Implement a simple *hashtag* to track the conversation. Hashtags are tracking tools that allow you to identify tweets and other postings under a quick-to-find category in any search engine or platform-specific search. You can find out more about hashtags and what to do with them in Chapter 13, where we cover best practices.

Now that we have completed an audit of our first impression and have taken a closer look at the anatomy of a tweet, where do we go from here?

Twitter is my go-to social media platform because it's fast. I have connected with industry professionals as well as readers through short tweets, and being able to make different lists to sort the people I follow helps me to manage the stream of information. I appreciate being able to filter the information myself, rather than miss out on posts due to an algorithm like Facebook tends to do.

—LISA KESSLER, AMAZON BEST-SELLING AUTHOR

BEST PRACTICES FOR TWITTER

Establishing and evaluating a presence on Twitter is not simply based on the amount of followers or how often you tweet. There are a multitude of live Twitter accounts, and many, many authors populate their Twitter feeds with the good, the bad, and the downright ugly. What you should strive for is a Twitter feed that offers content relevant to you and your interests.

The first thing you should do *before your book comes out* is to launch your Twitter account. Build your platform and become part of the community in advance of using it to market your book and your writing.

Remember that Twitter is about community and interaction. Keep your feed interesting and lively by talking about things *other than your book*. Share images of places you travel to. Tweet a beneficial resource that you just discovered. Post a quick review of a movie you just watched. People want to get to know you, so little updates of your life are as important as your writing. It's your choice how much you want to share, and you should set boundaries for yourself, but talking about your book *and only your book* will get very old very quickly. Aim for one "buy my book" tweet every five to ten tweets. Show people you want to connect and communicate with them, not just sell yourself and your books.

While building your network and tweeting with others, seek out and follow other writers, publishers, and agents. Before following them, however, look at their feeds. See if they are actually having conversations with people or simply talking *at* their networks. Avoid the "Let me tweet to you how *awesome* my books are" feeds, and focus more on those who tweet about good writing mixed with tweets of a personal nature. Depending on the quality of his conversations, a professional author's Twitter feed serves as a great way to listen in on what is happening in the market place. Twitter can also keep you in the know concerning which agents are looking for new clients, what publishers are seeking from the slush pile, or the latest on publishing scams.

Screening Twitter feeds is a great way to assure your network is built on quality as opposed to quantity. Sure, there are writers on Twitter who have tens of thousands (or even hundreds of thousands) of followers, but how well are they actually connecting with their networks? What is the worth of a Twitter feed that is nothing but constant retweets, posting of famous quotes, and incessant "Buy My Book Now!!!" links? Check out each person who follows you, and only follow back those who are actual people. You may find your numbers will climb much slower, but you will build a Twitter network that is responsive, receptive, and reliable.

Speaking of a responsive, receptive, and reliable network, make a note of this priority for your Twitter feed—*reply to mentions.* Watch your feed, and when a mention comes in, provided it comes from a real person and not a spambot (one of those pesky automated systems that spits out tweets), send a reply to that person. This is how communication begins, and you never know what will lead to a new reader.

For fans who tweet, you're guaranteed to make their day with a simple "Thank you for reading my book" tweet. Even writers like Neil Gaiman (@neilhimself) will occasionally respond to followers.

These are, of course, the *best* practices for Twitter. What about the worst? It stands to reason that if you have authors who are connecting with networks, making sales, closing deals, and moving forward in their careers, you have writers who are continuously making terrible decision after terrible decision on Twitter, not caring about the damage it does to their brand or their book.

YOU DID NOT JUST TWEET THAT: *WORST* PRACTICES FOR TWITTER

It takes patience to build a quality network, but you can easily torpedo a Twitter account (not with the occasional slip-up—no one is perfect, and Twitter is proof of that) with continuously bad behavior and thoughtless actions that can severely undermine whatever sense of community you're trying to establish.

THE BIGGEST, MOST COMMON MISTAKE authors make on Twitter is turning their account into one giant infomercial about their book. Every tweet—*every single tweet*—is a tweet about their book, sometimes ten to twenty tweets in a day. They may be written in such a fashion that Twitter will not automatically flag them as spam, but a constant stream of links to a book and how scary-awesome it is fails to build a community around that author or his book.

THE SECOND MOST COMMON MISTAKE authors make on Twitter is to beg for followers. You may receive a mention thanking you for the follow, immediately followed by a request for you to like the person's Facebook page. The worst is when you receive an automatic Direct Message asking you for a Like. Desperation isn't attractive in any situation and makes you look unprofessional. Get to know your network on Twitter. If they like what you have to say, they will find you on your blog, Facebook, or elsewhere. Trolling for followers is just tacky.

Equally tacky tactics include:

- Misrepresenting yourself in your bio. We once had someone follow us who described himself in his bio as a "best-selling author" when his debut novel was to come out later that year.
- Filling your Twitter feed with inspirational quotes from other books and authors. People follow you to hear what you have to say, not to revel in the wisdom of others.

SOCIAL MEDIA FOR WRITERS

- Filling your Twitter feed with inspirational quotes from your books or yourself. Don't let success go to your head. You're not that important; keep yourself in check.
- Filling your Twitter feed with nothing but retweets. Retweeting is not participation or engagement. It can be part of it, but nothing but retweeting is regurgitation. Indulge in retweets, but don't make them your only source of content.
- Following people only to drop them later the same day. Many third-party applications and services that promise you more followers will follow other Twitter accounts. Once the followed reciprocate, they are immediately dropped off your feed. It is not against Twitter's terms of service, but it is highly unethical. This is one way third-party developers turn social media into a pursuit of statistics, analytics, and numbers, something we will discuss more in detail in Chapter 13 of this book.

Authors behave badly on Twitter in many ways, but it is a good idea to practice the same etiquette you would practice in the real world, such as when pitching ideas to agents and editors upon meeting them. At an event, would you walk up to an agent or editor and say, "I have an idea you must look at!" without introducing yourself or asking if they are accepting pitches? Probably not, but it happens often on Twitter. Get to know these individuals as both professionals and people. Find out who is looking and what they want. Never pitch to editors or agents online unless you've been invited to do so.

I find Twitter absolutely indispensible for getting news fast and first. If you want to know who's looking for what when, who's been promoted or moved to another company, what line has closed or expanded ... there's a good chance you'll hear of it on Twitter before anyone else. It's a great way to keep on top of what's current.

—LUCIENNE DIVER, AUTHOR OF THE VAMPED
AND THE LATTER-DAY OLYMPIANS SERIES

By applying these basic approaches and strategies to your profile and the composition of your tweets, and working on what to do and what to avoid, you can make your Twitter account a very powerful platform. At this point, you should invest some time in Twitter. Get comfortable with the approaches we outlined in this chapter. Apply these methods and watch how the interaction between you and your network improves. All that remains now is building on your reputation and making your Twitter account a community, one that doubles as a team of promoters dedicated to the success of your works.

Facebook and Twitter are often referred to as cornerstones of a strong social media presence, but as you can see in this book, there are plenty of other platforms out there to employ. Let's turn to a social media platform with, many consider, the greatest unrealized potential. This social network not only offers many features and potential reach of SEO (search engine optimization, covered in greater detail in Chapter 11), but it also has without a doubt the biggest helicopter parent powering it. Yes, it's time to talk about Google+.

CHAPTER 6

Google+

A Place for Discussions and Hangouts

Facebook is the go-to place for posts, images, and video in social media, but not to be outdone, Google offered an alternative in 2011. Many online tech critics predicted it might be the "Facebook Killer" at its launch, with membership skyrocketing to half a billion active users before the end of 2013. However, *Google Plus* (also known as *G+* and *Google+*) has spent much of its existence attempting to develop an identity. Google spent the summer of 2015 reimagining the platform, but Google+, as is, still offers writers different ways to reach readers.

Google+, on its arrival, promised it would be a one-stop service where updates and blog posts could be posted and syndicated; photos could be uploaded, displayed, and shared across networks; and discussions from inside and outside a person's network could be hosted over distributed links, images, and media. Google+ and Facebook seem to mirror one another, but Google+'s seamless integration with the world's most popular search engine grants the unassuming, underestimated network boundless potential, both as a contender against Facebook and an outlet for authors. Its demographics lean toward professional males, and these males tend to be interested in discussions rather than images, which dominate Tumblr and Pinterest. So if your genre and topic are of interest to this group, then Google+ could be the place to grow your brand.

As of the writing of this book, the future of Google+ is somewhat nebulous. Changes in Streams, Hangouts, Photos—separating them into individual products—have people trumpeting the death of the social media platform as a whole. Bradley Horowitz, the Google executive in charge of the product said at a press event, "Google+ will be changing. There's a renaissance in the thinking of what Google+ is, and what it's for."[1] Just what all this will translate into down the line even we as writers of the fantastical cannot say. We will, however, continue to monitor the situation and blog about it on onestopwritershop.com.

GOOGLE+ FOR WRITERS: THE ACCOUNT VS. THE PAGE

If you are one of over 500 million active users with a Gmail account, you already have a Google+ account waiting for you. All you need to do is post a suitable profile picture, a quick bio, and a few facts about who you are and where you live to complete your account—all very much in line with social networking platforms like Facebook and Twitter.

That is how you set up a personal account on Google+. When establishing a Google+ *Page*, you must take a different approach.

When you set up a Page, you are immediately treated as a business. Are you establishing a Page as a Google+ *Storefront*, a *Service*, or a *Brand*? (Authors would fall under the "Brand" distinction.) Creating your Page is a simple process, at first. Give a name to your Page, a website providing more information on your future content, and a Brand that describes what type of business you are. Details such as a Profile Photo, Cover Photo, and Story are all that are needed to complete your Google+ Page. You now have your platform up and running.

---

1 http://www.cnet.com/news/google-plus-will-be-changing-says-its-chief/

BOOKMARK

What about a *Google+ Community* based around you and your works? Wouldn't that work as well as a Google+ Page?

Go back and take a look at the Facebook chapter's section on *Groups*. A Google+ Community works the same way, built around a cause, a common interest or, in the case of writers, a genre or series. The content found in a community is completely driven by its members, and this would mean either you join a community similar to yours—setting yourself up as a potential spammer if you come in hammering promotions about your material—or you host a community, which will take some time to build, provided its membership contributes.

And keep in mind, in a Google+ Community, everyone participates. Content is provided by the users and, even if the host of the community posts, other community participants can post and bury your promotional posts. Additionally, if it is your Community, you must serve as Moderator, adding to your responsibilities in managing Google+.

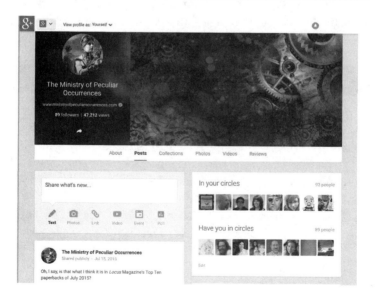

On Facebook, your followers—whether on your Page or on your personal account—tend to blur the lines between your personal and professional identity. Google+ takes a very different approach to followers. From any account you establish, Google+ grants you the ability to set up *Circles* for those you are following and those who are following you. Circles can be labeled with any distinctive name you give them, and by organizing your followers into these Circles, you can then target your posts to the public feed, to your network (or Circles) only, or to specific Circles in your Google+ accounts. Organizing your followers into Circles allows you to target your posts as exclusive content or private content you wish to share only with certain people. In other words, you can control where your message goes and how wide your posts or media is distributed.

Circles can also be established and managed in a Page similar to a personal Google+ account. Accounts are then managed by anyone who has access to your Google+ account. If you are security conscious, you may not want to reveal your credentials to fans helping you out with your "street team," which we will talk about in Chapter 13. Essentially, street teams are made up of fans who spread the word about your book. Google+ allows you to select the *Managers* tab from the *Settings* tab of your page to set your preferences.

BOOKMARK

If you followed the Appendices and created a Page, you should when you return to the Google+ main feed (the Stream), you are not liking, commenting, or sharing as yourself anymore. You are now interacting with the Google+ community as your Page. When creating your Page in Google+, much like in Facebook, you either do so as "Tee Morris, author," "The Writing Worlds of Philippa Ballantine," or "The Ministry of Peculiar Occurrences." Doing this creates a distinction between your personal account and your professional page, which allows readers to easily follow you.

Managers, when posting and administering Pages, will have access to a *My Business* panel option in their left-hand drop-down menu. My Business features not only a posting interface, but also *Insights* (a breakdown of the activity on the page), direct access to *Google Analytics* (a measurement tool for traffic coming to and from websites, demographics, and overall online content performance), and the one-click option for starting a *Hangout,* online gatherings that usually involve Google+'s ability to easily host video conferences (more on Hangouts later). From this dashboard, you can post content, consult with statistics on both your account and main website, and host Hangouts. This makes Google+ convenient and easy to add into your social media routine.

So far the capabilities of Google+ make the platform sound a lot like Facebook and, truth be told, it is. On its minimalistic surface, the Google+ graphic user interface looks a lot like Facebook in how it works and how you interact with it … at least on the surface.

Dig just a little deeper and you witness the firepower of this fully *armed* and *operational* social network!

Fire at will, Commander.

Oh, sorry about that. Geek moment. Let me try this again.

Dig a little deeper and you begin to tap into the full integration of Google, which is kind of like a Death Star, just not with the whole "blowing up planets" thing.

The Beginning of a Beautiful Friendship: Other Google+ Options

It could be very easy to dismiss your Google+ account as merely Facebook Lite, but now that you have set up a Page, you can easily go beyond what you have in front of you and start tapping into the potential of the world's largest search engine. Your Google+ account offers seamless integration that can provide your social media platform dynamic content and collaborative options.

YOUTUBE: A two-way street is a wonderful thing. When someone comments on your YouTube video, it posts automatically to your Google+ account. Then, when you reply (either as yourself or from your Page) with your Google+ account, it posts back to YouTube. It's the little things that make life easier.

HANGOUTS: Perhaps one of the most appealing content-creation tools in Google+'s arsenal, and now in yours, is the *Hangout*, which is seamlessly integrated with another Google property, YouTube. A Google Hangout is a video chat that can host ten different users, all of whom can join in on the topic at hand. The video signal remains on the person talking, so you will see the camera jump from participant to participant, especially when the conversation gets lively. The whole Hangout can then be recorded and uploaded to YouTube as a vlog entry. On YouTube, the video can be distributed either to private audiences (making the Hangout exclusive content) or to a wider, more public audience (making it new content for current and potential readers to consume).

Before diving headlong into hangouts, make sure you have a decent microphone (no problem if you are into podcasting as well) and, if you want to take advantage of the video option, a reliable camera. Make sure to set aside some time to host a test Hangout with a few friends so you know which buttons to push and how to switch from camera to desktop sharing if you want to make your Hangout even more interactive.

Though the changes going on in Google+ are still unfolding, one thing is certain: Hangouts will remain. This feature is one of the most beloved of all of the integrated options in Google+. That means it is probably a safe bet for you as an author to investigate.

There are many ways to use Google Hangouts. Imagine getting nine dedicated readers in a Hangout for an hour and chatting with them about your book. Think about how you could do giveaways during that time. It also gives readers a chance to get to know you as more than just a name on the cover of a book. This kind of Hangout could be a great way of interacting with your most passionate readers or making a passing reader a committed fan. Those who do not actually get into the Hangout can still participate in a chat room forum. Find a time to suit your schedule, and try one out. If you find it enjoyable, then consider making it a regular thing. As your following grows, you can vary the participants in the Hangout so everyone gets a chance. Use a signup form for those who are interested.

A launch party on Hangouts is a great way to get more face-to-face interaction with your readers, without having to jump on a plane. You could invite a select group into a Hangout, or if you have a network of writers, you could have them come to a Hangout and celebrate. Talk about your feelings, and, heck, even trepidations, as your book is launched into the world. Alcoholic beverages and finger food are optional.

Another option is to create a more general book group. For this group, you would contribute to book culture and promote authors other than yourself. A great example of this is a group led by author, actress, and all-around Internet entrepreneur Felicia Day. Vaginal Fantasy Book Club is a fun, monthly Hangout with a light "sitting down for a chat with the girls" feeling. During the Hangout, participants review, between sips of wine, romance genre books featuring female protagonists. However, they are not afraid to wander from the topic and get in a few laughs, either. Once the discussion is done, the Hangout is exported directly to YouTube, instant content for the VFBC's popular Goodreads Group that continues the chat until the next monthly Hangout. This Goodreads group is very popular, numbering fourteen thousand members all watching the current Hangout video.

Google may have pulled Google+ in for some behind-the-scenes tinkering, but one of its products is still the big man on campus as far as video goes. Google bought YouTube back in 2006, and that seems to have been a wise move on the company's part.

CHAPTER 7

YouTube
Introducing Video to Your Content

The platforms previously discussed in this book—Facebook, Twitter, Google+, WordPress—have mostly dealt with promoting content in text form. Yes, as an author, reading is the preferred format—we create worlds with our words while the readers fill in the blanks with their imagination. So it really should not come as a surprise when authors, plotting and planning out their social media initiatives, do not necessarily take into account visual platforms, and when it comes to visual platforms, none stands taller than *YouTube*.

With over a billion people using YouTube, four billion views of YouTube daily, and 323 days worth of video viewed through Facebook every minute, it is a wonder that more authors are not taking advantage of the video platform. Sure, there are a number of how-to videos and (of course) cats and dogs doing deliriously cute stuff, but how does that reflect or even represent the business of books? How compelling would video clips of someone writing be? When you think about it from that perspective, it makes perfect sense that authors—an introverted bunch, on the whole—do not feel that YouTube is the place for them.

And there are a few other factors that may deter authors from considering YouTube.

Camera Time

If you think authors look awkward or uncomfortable in still shots, try getting them in front of video cameras. Addressing a camera and talking to it in a casual, relaxed manner can be admittedly awkward, and that's coming from an author who used to be a card-carrying, dues-paying member of the Screen Actors Guild. There is a definitive personality who enjoys getting in front of a camera and talking in a conversational tone, and most authors do *not* fall into that category.

Production Details

You may think "A YouTube video? Piece of cake. Point. Shoot. Post. How hard can it be?" When you take a look at authors who know how to make YouTube work for them (and, yes, we're looking at you, Vlog Brothers[1]), consider what these video barons all have in common.

Take note of the background. Chances are, it is a library or a neutral background. Listen to the sound quality. What you hear probably is not coming from the microphone on the camera, but a lavalier mic that you can't see and that has been synced with the video in post-production. What about the lighting? Is the video lit in an atmospheric manner, or is it shot *au naturel?* You want to be able to be easily seen and at the very least convey a mood. What is the author wearing? How does her skin tone appear? Are the edits simple cuts or transitions, or are they peppered with bullet points that drive the intent of the episode home? All of these details when *not* considered reflect in the tone of the video and reduce it to something akin to *The Blair Witch Project,* or what is more commonly referred to as *guerrilla-style* video. With guerilla-style video, the production elements are kept to the basics: enough light to see what you are recording, wardrobe goes with the moment, and if you happen to be wearing makeup, you're good. Guerilla style is totally unscripted, off-the-cuff, point-and-shoot video, so keep it brief. You can make

---

1 https://www.youtube.com/user/vlogbrothers

a video-in-the-moment work, but you still need a plan. That kind of planning is essential to success on YouTube.

That brings us to another issue with authors entering the world of video.

Time

All of the following require time: Setting up a camera or multiple cameras; making sure the light is adequate; creating a slick, clever opening sequence; creating an end sequence where people can learn how to subscribe to your channel; and finally, editing. There are social media gurus who claim there are ways to cut corners that will save you some time. One of those corners is editing.

Before you agree with that sentiment, think about that—no editing. Would you consider forgoing editing when it comes to your book? Think about the draft you completed prior to editing. Editing is an essential part of a book's life, and with video it is even more critical as you deal with outtakes, missed beats, and tangents, all of which need to be trimmed down to the core of your message.

Time remains one of the biggest reasons authors stay off YouTube. You want your video to look good. No, it will not be the same quality as, say, a film from Marvel Studios; but you do want it to be a step above *America's Funniest Home Videos*.

BOOKMARK

Here's a formula that's pretty accurate: The time it takes to edit video is one hour for every finished minute of video. So if you have a ten-minute video, you will be looking at ten hours of editing, provided you do not have any additional filming, animation, or media to import into the project.

If you recall, in Chapter 3, we talked a bit about the commitment you make when podcasting. Video takes that commitment level to a much higher plane. Even with a twenty-year background in video editing, like Tee has, working in video can be a time-consuming and budget-consuming endeavor. While you can pick up a laptop computer for a drop in the bucket of what it takes to actually produce video footage, it is unlikely your machine will possess the processing power needed to render and output video on its own. (No, watching Netflix on your computer is not the same as creating your own production.) This is why computers are made bigger, stronger, faster—because in order to handle creative opportunities like this, you need bigger, stronger, and faster. Video is costly on a lot of levels, and while we have both enjoyed what we have accomplished with video editing and YouTube, we still hesitate to encourage authors to give YouTube a go.

Still want to do it?

It's not too late to turn back.

Okay then.

Lights, camera …

ACTION EDITING: SOFTWARE FOR VIDEO EDITING

If you were to do a search on the Internet for programs on video editing, you would find yourself with an impressive list of options for Macs, PCs, and Linux for those writers who are truly passionate about their operating systems. We don't intend to go into every software package available for all platforms here, but we will spotlight the popular ones, as well as the editing suites that offer options and resources to reach out to and find answers to your questions in a timely manner. Each of these software packages has different interfaces, features, and add-ons, but all of them perform the basic function you need—editing video.

- **IMOVIE (MAC):** If you are editing video on a Mac, you are already in a community of creative types, as Apple remains prevalent in the creative sectors. iMovie comes with a variety of built-in transitions and animations you can add to your video, and it easily interfaces with iPhoto and iTunes for those who want to incorporate photos or music into their production. iMovie is intuitive, but there are many online resources and print tutorials available for the higher functions available with its interface. iMovie is an amazing application for its $14.99 price tag—if you buy a new Mac, you will get it for free.

- **FINAL CUT PRO X (MAC):** iMovie is an amazing application, but depending on what you want to accomplish, you may find yourself reaching its limits quickly. If so, you need to make the jump from iMovie to Final Cut Pro X. The cost is considerably higher, though it has been recently reduced to $299.99. The upgrade goes well beyond the basics, although it uses a similar GUI to iMovie. Final Cut will take your video to the next production level, offering you many more options in how many tracks of video you can edit, advanced control over audio and video filters, and output options. While iMovie is a terrific, intuitive program, Final Cut comes with a learning curve that's not too steep but definitely requires time with the how-to manual. You may want some of these advanced options for your YouTube channel. Others you may never need. It all depends on the demands of your video, whatever the project may be, and how deep you want to go with your post-production.

- **MOVIE MAKER (WINDOWS):** This editing suite is the iMovie for Windows. Some may argue that iMovie offers more, but that may not make much of a difference considering the end product of an author's video productions should be as simple and easy as possible. All you really need to do is edit, review, and post. Movie Maker offers AutoMovie Themes, which can give your video professional touches such as rolling credits, video effects, and even transitions. All of the above expedite the post-production process. As it is with iMovie, the program usually comes preinstalled with your computer.

- **ADOBE PREMIERE (WINDOWS AND MAC):** You've met iMovie's counterpart. Now meet Final Cut's. Adobe Premiere comes in two flavors: Elements and Pro. If you have worked with Adobe Photoshop Elements, then you have a good idea of what Premiere Elements offers: the basics of video editing. You have just what you need, at an affordable price, contained in one software package, and you have many more options at your fingertips than you would have with Movie Maker in transitions, prepackaged video templates, and video effects. Similar to Final Cut Pro, the set of features you desire from your editing suite depends on the demands of your video and how much production is involved.

- **AVS VIDEO EDITOR (WINDOWS):** AVS Video Editor offers the basics of Movie Maker, but with a simple, elegant interface similar to iMovie. Video Editor also offers the option to capture video off your desktop (great for tutorials and software walk-throughs, discussed later in this chapter) and produce an interactive DVD, complete with menu interfaces provided by the application. Video Editor runs on Windows platforms only and can be found online,[2] alongside other media production software packages.

- **OPENSHOT (LINUX):** OpenShot Video Editor is a free, open-source video editor for Linux first created in August 2008. OpenShot compiles videos, photos, and music with subtitles, transitions, and effects, just like its Windows and Mac equivalents. Similar to programs like Final Cut and Premiere, OpenShot allows you to create videos that can be loaded onto DVDs and online platforms like YouTube. What's different about OpenShot is its "open source" nature. As part of the Open Invention Network (OIN), OpenShot encourages developers to create their own add-ons and extensions that, after community testing, are offered to other editors. So if

---

2 www.avs4you.com

you are a writer and a developer, and you want to create a signature extension like a custom video effect or a template that can quickly make your videos uniform in some way for your fellow Linux users, OpenShot is your best option.

- **KDENLIVE (LINUX AND MAC):** Free and safe to download, Kdenlive is another multitrack video editor for Linux and Macintosh. Kdenlive, much like OpenShot and other open-source software packages, encourages its community of editors and developers to create the best tools for video production. Kdenlive offers transitions and effects, and exports the final project to common formats for DVDs and Internet playback (such as DV, HDV, mpeg2, and h264). As Kdenlive and OpenShot are both free, the choice between the two comes down to which interface best suits you and your needs.

- **CAMTASIA (WINDOWS AND MAC):** Camtasia can serve as your video editor, but it is known more for its ability to create video captures from a computer. Camtasia turns your monitor (or one of your monitors, if you have multiple monitors for your computer) into the camera and records all your movements and commands or whatever activity is happening on your computer. This allows you to create *walk-throughs* (animated screen tutorials) of favorite computer programs. Many gamers use Camtasia to create walk-throughs of popular video games, offering helping hands for trickier challenges. Camtasia is easy to master and outputs to a variety of resolutions and formats for final video projects. It can be your stand-alone video editor or a great addendum for your video projects.

Whether you decide to go all in for a professional-grade video editor or keep your wallet happy and work with something that's cost-free, you will want to have one of these editing suites to make your video concise and as polished as possible.

When it comes to background music that you want to mix into your production, copyright laws are in effect. Your YouTube video is being used for promotional purposes, and your favorite song or soundtrack cut is not allowed. Even if you adopt the attitude of "Well, not that many people are watching …," you are still violating copyright. (Think of it as someone using passages of your book to promote her own image, website, or business without your permission.) Apart from original music, your option is *royalty-free music*, music that you pay for permission to use. The disadvantage is that multiple people can use the same royalty-free music, so you may hear your theme on another podcast or even a television commercial. The advantage? Royalty-free music, found on websites like Audiojungle. net, Beatsuite.com, and iStockphoto.com, is affordable and adds a touch of professionalism to your production. *Layered* royalty-free music, such as the collections at SmartSound.com, offers the versatility of being able to edit the music, thereby creating endless combinations from one track.

While there are plenty of successful vlogs that keep their details simple and basic, even the basics still take up time. Perhaps the most important detail to consider is why you are establishing a presence on YouTube. Without a direction, YouTube is no different than a story that plods along with no resolution or point in sight.

Time to ask the hard question: What do authors bring to YouTube?

TURNING AUTHORS ON TO YOUTUBE

Despite all our warnings and precautions about venturing into YouTube, video production is also infinitely rewarding. An engaging video not only reflects positively on your brand, but it also provides book bloggers and enthusiastic fans content that livens up any blog post or

Facebook status. What is paramount in establishing a YouTube presence is planning what you want to bring to your channel.

Beyond working on a keyboard and the odd book signing or two, though, it's hard to picture what is "visual" in an author's lifestyle. However, similar to Instagram (which we will talk about in Chapter 9), the potential for visual content might surprise you.

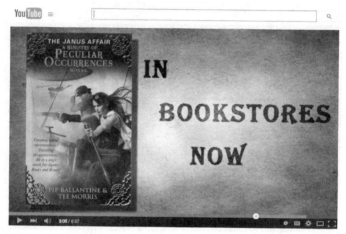

Steampunk Book Trailer — The Janus Affair: A Ministry of Peculiar Occurrences Novel

 Tee Morris

Book Trailers

Mention "video" to an author, and usually the first thing that comes to mind is *book trailer*. The purpose of a book trailer is no different than a movie trailer: You are promoting a book or a series. Making book trailers can be a daunting task, even if you keep it simple. There are challenges in finding stock video that fits your book's story. There are challenges in filming original content. The end results—examples found on "Being Kenneth Branagh: 11 Tips on Filming Book Trailers"[3] —should feel cinematic, not like animated PowerPoint presentations. They provide terrific promotional content for your books, so long as

---

3 http://bit.ly/filming-trailers

the production does not become too involved, and are easy to share across blogs and social networks ... However, when you factor in actors, location shots, and crew, making a trailer can easily become a lot to manage.

Author Appearances

This does not necessarily mean "book signings," as appearances can include conference appearances, panel discussions, and special events. You can offer a quick clip, or a series of clips, from a panel discussion. You can hold a quick commentary from the hallways of a writers conference or convention—this can be your thoughts from the event, "man on the street"–type interviews with attendees, or a bit of both. What if you host a book launch for your fantasy novel at a Renaissance faire? Capture moments of special guests, festivities, and (provided the turnout is there) book signings. Keep your mind open to special events and the content you can post. These moments serve as your invitation to others to enjoy the event alongside you.

Video Journaling

This is where an author takes a moment out of his day to get a thought or a moment recorded. If you are using YouTube, you should preserve these thoughts on video. It may be something completely writing related ("Use the audio recorder on your smartphone to jot down ideas when you are behind the wheel") or it could be more about lifestyle ("When was the last time you completely unplugged from your writing and just relaxed?"). Journal entries can be some of the most honest, sincere moments you share with your community. When you journal, make sure you are working within your comfort zones. Don't share too much (YouTube is not your therapist's couch), but don't be afraid to let your audience into your head. You do it all the time with your books. Why not do it with your video entries? This is where your YouTube channel feels closest to *vlogging*.

As the second largest search engine on the Internet, YouTube is not to be ignored.

I can get creative with my content on YouTube by posting in various forms: from personal vlogs on my writerly process (#PiperNotes) to cinematic book trailers to creating videos on topics that may be tangential to my writing (#PiperTravels) but that lead to plot bunnies!

Such a broad scope of possibilities allows me to continually create new kinds of videos that can be embedded anywhere, including in guest blogs and news articles, and in that way, they can help spread my brand to new readers without my needing to custom code or worry about having higher-end hosting with more capable bandwidth.

It allows me to look out at my readers and speak directly to them, overcoming the challenges of physical distance.

—PJ SCHNYDER, AKA PIPER J. DRAKE, AUTHOR OF THE AWARD-WINNING THE LONDON UNDEAD SERIES AND *HIDDEN IMPACT: A SAFEGUARD NOVEL*

How-To Videos and Walk-Throughs

Recently, for our own vlog, we featured a video that wasn't necessarily a "writerly topic," but more a DIY project. We turned a wall of our studio into a dry-erase board, and we felt this qualified as something we wanted (and needed) to share with our writing community. How-to videos provide a good portion of the content on YouTube and can cover any number of topics. The best how-to videos are projects that may seem hard to do on first consideration but wind up being easy and simple to see to completion. Suitable subjects include reorganizing and remodeling your office, and organization tips for your print resources. Any home improvements you're undertaking for your writing career is definitely YouTube worthy.

Walk-throughs are like how-to videos, but they are staged and shot on your computer. Perhaps you want to host a quick walk-through of your favorite feature in your favorite word processor and project management tool, Scrivener. Or how about showing the tricks to making quick and easy promotional cards for upcoming signings or special appearances? With a program like the earlier mentioned Camtasia or AVS Video Editor, you can create a video to guide your viewers through software packages.

Now that you have a good idea what authors could bring to YouTube, you have to take a serious look at how you want to film your production. Whether it is a full-blown, costumed spectacle or a vlog documenting your latest conference appearance, what you are creating is a production, and it should be approached as such. You, as producer and director, need to plan out your YouTube show before a single word is spoken in front of a camera.

BEST PRACTICES ON YOUTUBE

There is a method to creating video, and these strategies and approaches are designed to keep things simple. These strategies are also starting points for you as a filmmaker and videographer. You may want to go beyond what we recommend, and that's okay, but it's best to walk before you run.

Keep Your Video Brief

When we say "brief," we mean at or around five minutes. As we mentioned in an earlier Bookmark, it usually takes one hour of editing for every finished minute of video. So you could be looking at five hours of work for a five-minute video. This is five hours of work only if you have a lot of edits, transitions, and effects you're adding into your video, but regardless of how much work you are putting into the production, you want to aim for five minutes as the sweet spot for your video's running time.

BOOKMARK

A free YouTube account gives users fifteen minutes for video clip length. Anything beyond that limit will not be approved for playback until you verify your account with Google for free.

If you want your production to go longer than the YouTube limits, and you don't want to hassle with verification (which includes registering a mobile number with Google), a popular alternative for sharable video is *Vimeo*.[4] While it's not as widely used as YouTube, Vimeo offers a variety of plans—including a free one—that grant users space for multiple videos, ad-free playback, and expanded options and customization for its user interface. If you find yourself in need of options beyond YouTube, take a closer look at Vimeo.

Keep the Video Editing Simple

In an application like iMovie, it is tempting to add in wacky filters and effects for pizzazz, but all these touches add time to making your production. Additional effects mean more *rendering time*—this is where the application produces a final, self-contained file that doesn't need the video editing software for playback but plays in any media player. How can you keep the demands of video production down? Keep the editing simple: Use basic cuts, eliminate transitions when and where you can, and don't use visually intensive effects. Have an introduction video, a simple sequence of segments and cuts, and a snappy, polished end screen.

Speaking of your introduction and end screen …

Dedicate time for the Introduction and End Screen

Create "bookends" for your production. Your video's Introduction should be the most "complicated" aspect of your production, maybe some animated titles (or still shots) and the title of your show. Create it as an individual project and output it as a video. There are several ways to create an End Screen (and YouTube has many tutorials, some that involve Camtasia). Once you have an Introduction and an End Screen, you have your two "bookends." In between, keep your pro-

---

4 http://vimeo.com

duction simple. With the complicated segments produced and any remaining segments lacking effects or animations, the rendering time should be quick.

Rehearsal Is Always a Good Thing

So are multiple takes. When the camera goes live, you may stumble on your words. Give yourself a beat, then start the thought again. This is why you edit—to remove the flubs and trips in your recording session. Before you even turn on the camera, speak your thoughts out loud. Hear yourself putting thoughts to speech. Think about how your tone or intent comes across. Then refine it before hitting record. The more comfortable you are with your thoughts, the smoother your words will sound and the more confident you will appear on screen; with video, confidence is key. Between rehearsing your thoughts and refining your final video with editing to remove stammers, pauses, and misfired thoughts, your final video will be an engaging production that promotes your brand.

Have Material Ready

Before launching your YouTube platform, produce five to ten episodes. If you want to get a better idea of the time commitment you are facing, produce five episodes, at the minimum. If you are feeling bold, produce ten episodes. When you are done, you'll have a buffer of episodes that you can post every other week (up to four months of material) or monthly (up to ten months). Don't go live with the YouTube platform just yet, but note the time and effort it has taken to create these episodes. Can you handle the time commitment? Are you ready to step into the YouTube arena? Knowing what goes into not just one episode, but a series of episodes, will help you allocate time for your channel.

YouTube remains mostly uncharted territory for authors, mainly because of the time commitment and financial investment. With the right strategy and creative thinking, though, YouTube can provide your audience with engaging, entertaining content that they'll want to share across multiple networks. Video editing is difficult but also very rewarding. Devise a plan and strategy for your YouTube channel, and see what happens. You may be surprised how much fun being in front of a camera can be.

Next you'll get away from the moving image and head over to Pinterest, where the long, vertical image is king.

CHAPTER 8

Pinterest
Your Online Bulletin Board

Think of all the corkboards in kitchens around the world, and all the postcards, recipes, and notes pinned onto them. Now wouldn't it be nice if you had an infinite corkboard for the Internet, where you could keep all those important, pretty, and interesting items? Wouldn't it be great if you could share your corkboard with your friends, and you could see all the fascinating things they found?

The creators of *Pinterest* must have thought so, too. They created Pinterest as a visual bookmarking site, where people collect and collate projects and ideas, and share them with others. Each user can have multiple boards where they post things that interest them.

When it was created in March 2010, Pinterest quickly became the hot topic among its target demographic, which is women. Everyone was talking about the inspiration that evolved from sharing items with their friends. They were getting ideas for birthday parties, delicious drinks, holiday decor. In a matter of months, Pinterest.com became a very busy, very active Web domain.

Think of Pinterest as a huge online bulletin corkboard, where users Pin images, websites, and videos to their "boards" for others to look at and gather inspiration. Users put together as many boards as they want, based on hobbies, vacations, fashion, books, or whatever topics interest them. It is a great way for users to keep track of items they want to return to all over the Internet. These Pins act as visual bookmarks—clicking on the image links to the original content or display original content from the board owner.

Collages scare me. What with the cutting, gluing, hot mess vomiting all over a board and maybe, *likely,* smeared with glitter. But the *idea* of collages has always intrigued me. Wouldn't it be great if I could gather inspirational art without, you know, the scissors and the paper cuts and the glue sniffing? Enter Pinterest! Inspired by a bit of art? Pin it! That thing looks like the zombies I'm writing about? Click, saved! Love that guy's … let's go with smile? Added! Now I can collage forever, and I get unlimited boards full of ideas and inspiration. Finally! Doing it freaking right.

—KARINA COOPER, AWARD-WINNING AUTHOR OF
THE ST. CROIX CHRONICLES

Out of all of the social media platforms, Pinterest's demographics are very unique, leaning heavily towards females in the thirty-five to forty-four age group. And, the average household income of an average Pinterest user is over $100,000. Pinners are not afraid of spending money, which is always a great demographic for markets. By 2013, Pinterest had become so popular that it was estimated that one-third of all women in America have used the site. So if you know your target audience is women, Pinterest is a social media platform you will need to have in your online arsenal. According to a recent study from the National Endowment for the Arts, 55 percent of women read fiction.

That is not to say men are not on Pinterest as well. The same study found that men are more likely to read *nonfiction* books. Having a Pinterest board of DIY projects related to your how-to manual could provide a terrific resource for those already reading your book, earn you new readers from men searching Pinterest for new ideas, and keep your book relevant by providing online addendums and new ideas.

Pinterest also sports a widely spread age demographic. However, as far as global reach goes, it is most popular in America—something that writers should keep in mind when deciding whether to add it to their marketing strategy. If your book is unavailable in the United States, then Pinterest is going to be of limited use to you. However, for independent authors taking advantage of a global reach, America is still a vital market.

While Pinterest may be one of the smaller social networks, with 70 million users worldwide in 2014, it does boast passionate "pinners" who spend a good amount of time on the site—15.8 minutes *per day*—

sharing information with each other and discussing their latest interesting discovery.

Another vital demographic trend about pinners is that they tend to take recommendations and buy from Pinterest; at last count, 47 percent of online shoppers have bought an item after a recommendation from Pinterest. Those are great statistics for selling books; other social media platforms would be excited to have stats that good.

In summary, Pinterest is the social media platform where well-off women of all ages seek out interesting content and are happy to purchase items of interest. This is why large brand names are flocking to Pinterest. Writers can take advantage of the site in the same way.

It's time to dive into the world of Pinterest and become part of its thriving community.

BOOKMARK

The best time to Pin is when the majority of your audience has time to relax with Pinterest. Analytics vary from category to category, but generally speaking, the best times are in the evening and on Saturday mornings. These, of course, need to happen in the standard North American time zones.

TOOLS OF THE TRADE: PINTEREST APPLICATIONS

Pinterest is best described as a virtual bulletin board, which elicits an unassuming image, but don't be fooled. There's a lot happening there. Once you establish your profile and get all your details online, it is best to explore and (subsequently) master the nuts and bolts of your Pinterest account. While there are a few features and options worth mentioning, the good news is they are extremely user-friendly.

BOOKMARK

As we are eight chapters deep into this book, you may see a pattern when it comes to your profiles and accounts. You want your usernames, profiles, and profile pictures to all follow the same look and feel so that when you tell people "You can find me online at ...," you only have to give one screen name. If you do find yourself in need of creating new profile names for yourself, the reoccurring profile picture and simple bio will let people know they have found you. When it comes to profiles, adhere to the two Cs: *completion* and *consistency*.

The Bookmarklet

There is one piece of useful equipment you should have before you begin pinning in the wilds of the Internet. Go to the website[1] and then click on Install Now. The Pin button goes in your browser and makes pinning things on the Web much easier. Now when you click on the Pin It button, you will find a selection of the images that you can Pin. Choose the best one, click to Pin, then add a description.

The Widget

In order to spread the word about your pinning activity, the site offers a widget that can be placed on your blog. It comes in a square, header, or sidebar, or can even be customized to fit your particular situation. It is a great way to let people know that you are on Pinterest. On our websites, we usually have it right in the header so it is immediately apparent.

To find this widget, you can simply go to Pinterest.[2]

The Mobile App

Pinterest has a great app for on-the-go pinning from your smartphone. The app is available for both Android and OSX. You can find it in their stores or download it.[3] Anything you can do on the Pinterest website, you can do on your smartphone. The only negative is that it's hard to zoom in on images, but that is a minor problem. You get the full stream of the boards you are following, and after clicking on

---

1 http://about.pinterest.com/goodies/#browsers
2 https://business.pinterest.com/en/widget-builder
3 https://about.pinterest.com/en/goodies

any of them, you can repin straight to your boards—including any secret ones (which we'll discuss later in this chapter). You also have the "heart" functionality to like it, send it, and post it to other networks. In addition, you get the choice of saving the picture to your phone or simply copying the link. This is useful if you are writing a blog post on the subject while you're out and about. You also get access to the Pin logo, search, the bubble icon for chatting and news, and access to all your boards under the human head and shoulders icon. For more about what these features offer, go to the Pinterest appendix.

With these basic tools under your belt, you can accomplish a lot with Pinterest, but how? Sure, you can Pin your book cover, inspirational artwork, and images from your various events, but what will bring people to your boards and keep them there—preferably for longer than 15.8 minutes a day?

GAME ON: PINTEREST COMPETITIONS

Pinterest has become one of the go-to sites for winning items, since the Pinterest terms of service are actually more flexible than a lot of other social media networks—and they don't try and charge you for the privilege of promotion. Pinterest is happy for pinners to use their boards for promotion, as long as the pinners don't say Pinterest is running the competition. However, you must be strategic with competitions—don't run them all the time. Use pinning contests for marking important events, like book releases or holidays, or for making bestseller lists! You might do a Pin/repin to win a copy of your new title when it is released or a book in the wild competition for when you hit a bestseller list.

Calculate how much money you can afford to spend on a contest. The larger the prize, the more entries and reach you are likely to have. Keep in mind the interests of Pinterest users, and keep what you are asking them to do relatively simple. Nothing is more frustrating for a reader than jumping through hoops.

Before deciding what sort of contest you want to run, settle on your goal. Are you trying to get more people to your website? Do you want to get more subscribers to your e-mail list? Or are you just trying to increase book sales?

Pin/Repin to Win Competitions

These competitions are a good idea if you want to increase your number of Pinterest followers.

First, create a bright, attractive image of what your pinners are going to win. The image should contain your cover image if you are giving away something like a Kindle Fire. It should also say "repin to win" and use some variation of the word *competition* to draw attention and let visitors know they can get something for free. It's important to include a tempting description with keywords, as well as the value of the prize that is up for grabs, and a call to action like "post this," "repin this," or "take a picture of your own copy." In the description, make sure to say how a winner will be chosen, and the date the winner will be announced. Also keep an eye on Pinterest's terms and conditions (which are constantly being updated), just so you don't break any rules.

BOOKMARK

A lot of marketing suggests using the tag "Pin it to win it," but Pinterest rules specifically ask you not to. Why remains a mystery, but it is best to stick with other wording to remain compliant with your fine hosts.

Create a Wish List Board

Run a competition asking pinners to create a "wish list" board with your book on it, along with other books of a similar genre. Ask them to include a hashtag so you can find who has created the lists. This is especially good as it encourages friends and family of the pinner to purchase the book for them. At the end of the promotion, give away something of a decent dollar value, like a Kindle. You can choose a winner randomly, or judge the boards and pick a winner.

Books in the Wild

Build buzz for your book release by asking pinners to post pictures of the book in the wild, out in bookstores or with the readers themselves. All those Pins appear in their friends' feeds, hopefully resulting in more followers and greater awareness of your book. Again, post simple rules and create a hashtag so you can find the entries.

These are just some ideas for competitions. If you can dream up a contest, and it fits within the Pinterest terms of service, you should roll it out on a small scale and see what kind of response you get.

IT'S BUSINESS TIME: PINTEREST BUSINESS

As an author, you are a business, and Pinterest Business offers layers of depth that go above and beyond individual accounts. It is probably a good idea that you become familiar with the basics of the individual site before you jump into converting to a business account, but once you do, the options are thrilling.

The first step you must take is to go to Pinterest's business website[4] and convert your account. You need to have your own website to be verified. In order to do this you need to insert the code Pinterest gives you into the header, *<head>*, section of the HTML or where your blog template allows you to access that section of code. Pinterest shows you how to do this,[5] and it isn't difficult even if you don't know HTML. In exchange for a little bit of work, you will get some large advantages.

The first of these is undoubtedly Pinterest analytics. Pinterest supplies you with graphics about your Pinterest profile, your audience, and even activity that came from your website.

---

4 https://business.pinterest.com/en
5 https://business.pinterest.com/en/confirm-your-website

Pinterest Profile

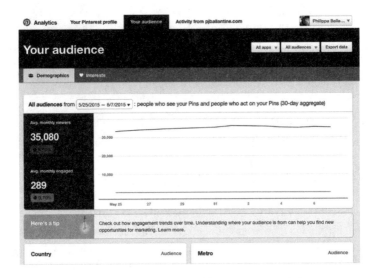

Here you can see your daily impressions (how often your page is loaded) and viewers for a whole year. It's always nice to be able to see trends and to observe how well your strategy is working. It will also give you the top Pin impressions and top boards with Pin impressions from the last thirty days, so you can see what images and videos are attracting pinners. Look for trends. Try to find what it is about your popular Pins that brings people to your boards. You can also access the same data on repins and clicks.

You can even break it down by the devices that people are using. Are your people Android users? You can easily find out, and it is useful for working out which sort of Pins are getting the most engagement.

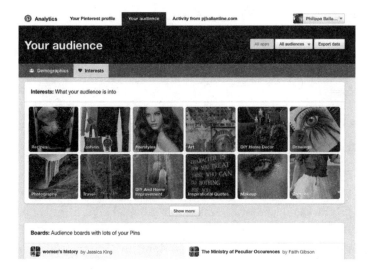

Your Audience

Once you've seen information about your Pins, you can find out more about those who viewed them, such as how engaged they are, which country they live in, their gender, their language, their metro area, and even what subjects they are interested in. The online trends and behaviors of Ministry of Peculiar Occurrences pinners, for example, have indicated that they are fond of recipes, fashion, art, and DIY home decor.

BOOKMARK

Analytics will have you register a site and verify it. Once that's done, it will track how many views you are getting from blog posts pinned to your boards. Then you will be able to see which are your top blog post Pins. Those Pins should give you some idea of what your board followers find most interesting. Take note of those posts' images and keywords, and use them in future posts to get the most views.

Activity from Your Site

How many viewers go to your website, and which Pins and boards are taking them there? Study those successful Pins and boards, and see what you can do to make your other Pins and boards equally as successful.

Other Business Tools

Pinterest Business accounts offer advantages outside of analytics as well.

- **PIN IT BUTTON:** This is useful if your website host doesn't have the button integrated into posts. Tumblr, Blogger, WordPress, and Wix all should, however. This button provides a quick and simple way for readers to Pin your post.
- **PROMOTED PINS:** Pinterest is working on a way to pay to promote your Pins. Initially, it will offer this service to U.S.-based businesses only.
- **WIDGETS:** Pinterest gives you a good selection of widgets. Follow buttons, Pin It buttons, and widgets to show off your profile or your boards all come prepackaged (or can be custom-sized) and ready for your blog or website.
- **PINTEREST LOGO:** All different sizes and shapes are available for you to use on your marketing materials, both online and off.
- **BUSINESS PINTEREST NEWSLETTER:** This comes out weekly. Sign up for it.
- **RICH PINS:** This new innovation is still being developed. Currently there are five different types of Rich Pins: Article, Place, Recipe, Movie, and Product. All Rich Pins contain extra information about the Pin, but product Pins probably offer the most to a writer, since they can include pricing, where to buy, and availability. Pinners may also get notifications when the price drops more than 10 percent. Rich Pins require a little more technical skill since they must be meta tagged and tested, so authors may want help from a site developer. They also need to be approved by Pinterest. Still,

it will be interesting to see how these develop. To keep an eye on them for use in the future, go to Pinterest's developer website.[6]

WATCH WHERE YOU POINT THAT PIN: PINTEREST STRATEGIES

Pinterest strategies are all about making the most of the visual medium and the community. As a writer, you might think you don't have many visual resources to mine, but with a little creative thinking and the Internet at your disposal, you'll soon find it is easier than you think to fill up a board with some Pin-worthy pieces.

Readers love to crawl inside the mind of their favorite—or newly discovered—writer. So let them in!

Now Boarding: Book, Series, and Character Boards

Create a board for each of your books or series, and display your inspiration. Think of it as the bonus features to the book. Pin photos of locations that inspired the stories, costumes that you imagine the characters wearing, historical images (if your book is history based), reviews, podcasts, fan art, and book covers.

If you want to start pinning before your book comes out, make the board a secret one. When you are ready to announce the publication of your book, you will simply edit the board to be public and, *voila*, you have instant content for your readers! Check out the Appendix on Pinterest if you need help on creating a secret board.

If you want to go further, you can create boards for individual characters. Fill these boards with insights into who the characters are, including books they might want to read, fashions they'd wear, or even decor they would have in their apartment.

Readers also love a sneak peek behind the curtain: Traditional publishers might not let you reveal unfinished or draft cover images, but if you are self-publishing, you get to make these decisions. Consider pinning cover image ideas, drafts, or a list of movie stars you'd

---

6 https://developers.pinterest.com/rich_pins_overview/

hire to play the characters in a movie of your novel. You can even ask readers to comment on what they think.

As with any social media, you should make your boards attractive and reflective of yourself. Have one for characters, one for settings, and one for series, but also make boards dedicated to your other interests: fashion, cooking, travel, or something connected with your writing, like costuming or history. Different boards are a great way to show how diverse a person you are—don't be afraid to let your personality shine through.

In conjunction with making it look good, always ensure you only Pin quality material. Readers will know that you care about your content and will return for more. Make sure you use your Pinterest account for more than mere marketing. You'll also need content that you find on other boards. Content curating (dealt with in Chapter 12 of this book) is the latest strong trend, and it can help make your boards a go-to location for your readers.

From Literal to Figurative: Mood Boards

Other popular boards—like mood or color boards—can also be used to market your book. It is surprising how many pinners are looking for boards that have themes on feelings, rather than subjects. It is something a little out of the ordinary, appealing to different senses. For example, you might make a mood board for your horror novel and call it "Creepy." Then you'd fill it with things that frighten you. If your book is a romance novel, you might make a board called "Joy" and populate it with fun and beautiful images. Color boards are popular with designers, but they will only work for you if you create something that fits in with your book. If your words were colors, what would they be? These boards will attract DIY and fashion enthusiasts, and those people read, too.

In the case of mood or color boards, don't forget a good, strong description, with that all-important website URL in it. People looking for inspiration might be curious enough to follow it.

Secret Pins: Keep It Secret ... Keep It Safe ...

When you Pin, make sure it isn't a dump of content all at once. Don't simply log on once a week and Pin fifty posts in one go. This will be overwhelming for your followers. Some of your more important Pins may drift past them in all the clutter. Instead, spread your pinning activities over the course of the week.

Unfortunately, unlike other social media networks such as Facebook and Tumblr, there is no queuing or scheduling a set time to post Pins. This leaves the writer with a bit of a challenge, but there is a work-around to make things a little easier. To avoid the dreaded Pin dump, create a secret Pin board. It's just like making any other board.

When you drop into Pinterest, you can gather all the Pins you want to use, or even create your own, and Pin them to this secret board. Then, later on in the week, simply go to your secret board, click on the Pin, and then click on the pencil icon. Now you can move the Pin from your secret board to your public ones. The Pin will now appear only on the public boards. Spend a couple of minutes every day—we like to tick this task off using our mobile app while on the train—shifting a few over to public.

Tell Me About It: The Importance of Descriptions

No matter how pretty your image is, if your audience admires it and keeps going, you haven't sold a book. Make sure you offer a strong description to go with the relevant, original content you post. You can use snippets from your book, character sketches, or behind-the-scenes glimpses. Long descriptions are more engaging, and Pinterest allows you five hundred characters. So make the most of them, and don't forget to include a link in that description!

BOOKMARK

Images and infographics that make the best impression are vertical, tall, and boldly colored. When users are scanning down, the longer your image stays in their stream, the more likely they are to click on it.

Directing Traffic: Blogging for Pinning

Pinterest is a great place to do cover reveals, contests, and promotions. So don't forget to Pin your blog post about these—just make sure there is an image for Pinterest to find. When you Pin directly from the Pinterest website, or with the Bookmarklet, Pinterest will detect an image available and put it on your board.

If you are really stuck for ideas on what to post, a great tool is the InstaQuote app. You can take a pull quote from your post and quickly turn it into an image. It may seem a little strange to quote yourself at first, but it is an eye-catching option, especially on Pinterest.

So, from now on, make sure each blog post you write contains an image. Practice good Pinterest etiquette, even when not on Pinterest.

Group Boards

Here's a good one if you want to share information with a publicist, co-writer, or perhaps a personal assistant. Boards can be shared! When creating or editing, simply go to your board, click Edit, and add the e-mail of that person. Once she has accepted your invitation, she will be able to Pin to your board. A good example of this kind of board used for marketing is the Alliance of Indie Authors: Members Books. Here, all members have a chance to post their book links.

A similar shared page would work well for local writers groups or authors who share a genre. It's a fabulous way to build a sense of community.

Pinterest combines visual delight with information in a way that few other social networks do. It can be a great benefit for you as a writer and a marketer. So get pinning, but be warned: Once you get started, it can be quite addictive.

In the next chapter, we explore another visual platform—one that captures moments as they happen. Instagram is a smartphone photography app that allows you to post on its own network alongside other heavy hitters like Facebook and Twitter. Instagram generates a new image for its own network and you can easily post this altered photograph to Pinterest, supplying personal memories to your board.

But how does Instagram alter your images? We'll see you in the next chapter and let you in on this visual platform's power and appeal.

Instagram
Adding Photography to Your Arsenal

Facebook, Twitter, and Google+ all offer the ability to post photos along with your updates, and this is an option that authors take advantage of. In the past two years or so, you might have noticed that your social networks—particularly in their mobile versions—have been offering a variety of filters for your photographs. One filter makes your photo appear as if it were taken in the nineteenth century while another gives it the look of a Polaroid One-Step.

These creative options for photographs came about because of an unassuming app that took images from a smartphone's camera and allowed the user to give them a nostalgic look. Launched in October 2010 and now sporting a membership of 150 million members, *Instagram* took online photography in a *backwards* direction, granting its users the ability to take pristine, megapixel photos and turn them into 1970s-looking, antique, or cinematic photographs. You can add slick borders, quirky angles, and a variety of color effects to your photos, tag the location (using a process commonly known as *geotagging*) and even tag other Instagram members into your images.

BOOKMARK

You may have heard of *Vine*. This is a *video*-sharing service that focuses on the short form—the very short form. The length of Vines clock in at six seconds, less than half the length of Instagram's videos. It is a very popular app and has been used for everything from music events to newsworthy happenings to stop-motion animated advertisements. It makes sense that in 2012 Twitter bought the company, since Vines are very popular to tweet out. Twitter and Vines fit together perfectly. Instagram, in response to the popularity of Vine, now offers similar video features. You can make it a single, continuous shot or put together a series of segments into one clip. The final fifteen seconds of an Instagram video has the added advantage of offering filters, just as if it were a still photo.

What makes Instagram popular, though, does not end with the really neat special effects available to your smartphone's camera. Instagram grants you the ability to take advantage of networks outside of its own, taking one post and distributing it automatically across other networks.

PLATFORM MANAGEMENT: CONNECTING INSTAGRAM WITH OTHER SOCIAL NETWORKS

Back in our blogging chapter, we told you that certain plug-ins in WordPress and Tumblr allow your new blog post to instantly appear on Facebook, Twitter, and other social networking platforms. Instagram also offers this service. It's a great example of how mobile apps make the most of popular online platforms by maximizing the reach of various networks using one image, one post.

There are six social networks you can connect to your Instagram. The first three networks are covered in-depth in this book, so you should know what they are and how they fit into your social media strategy.

- **FACEBOOK**
- **TWITTER**
- **TUMBLR**
- **FLICKR:** Flickr, available as a smartphone app, a stand-alone desktop app, an option for photograph management tools, and as a website, offers digital scrapbooks for family and friends, for

networks you build, or for everyone on the Internet. Instagram plugs in directly to the photography network and creates a photo stream that posts your images and accompanying comment on your Flickr account.

- **FOURSQUARE:** With a membership of over forty-five million, the popular geotagging network Foursquare allows its members to share locations. Wherever you are, Foursquare lets your network—or anyone on the Internet—know where you are. While you can still use the Foursquare-powered Location option on Instagram without being an active member of the network, connecting your Foursquare to Instagram allows your posts to count as official "check-ins" for that location.

- **MIXI:** Based in Japan, this network offers many of the same services as Facebook, only with expanded options to keep your content private.

If you have not connected your networks to Instagram yet, the app will walk you through a log-in process. You'll have to make this connection only once unless you are switching from account to account. After you sync your social media networks to Instagram, you can share your posts across multiple networks with a single tap.

BOOKMARK

Note above where we say, "You'll have to make this connection only once unless you are switching from account to account." Tee, on working with other clients and their Instagram accounts, has discovered a limitation: There is no easy way to float from one account to another. You must log off and then log back on to Instagram. Also, when you have logged back on to Instagram under a different account, it is a good idea to check the additional platforms to make sure they are accessing the right account. Otherwise, you may be cross-posting personal photos onto accounts that are not your own. Always make sure your message is heading out on the intended channel.

For a smartphone app, Instagram offers a lot of choices: different filters, various networks, and still or moving images, all allowing you to tell a story of that specific moment. Writers thrive on Instagram. They post poetry, teasers of upcoming releases, and moments from book events. Instagram is a powerful app just by itself, but other developers are now offering their own apps to help writers tell their stories through this photographic platform.

BEYOND INSTAGRAM: THIRD-PARTY APPS

Throughout this book, we suggest avoiding third-party applications that simply copy-and-paste your message into other platforms. Automation is a good thing in moderation, but it should not be the only way you appear on other platforms. You want your network to know there is a real person at the end of these updates, tweets, and posts, someone who is accessible and open for engagement.

Instagram is an exception to this rule. There are many third-party apps available geared specifically for Instagram or for the photographs and video on your smartphone to make them like and comment magnets for other Instagrammers.

PhotoGrid

It's one thing to post a truly breathtaking picture on Instagram, but what if you are in the middle of a book event and can't take a break to post it? Or what if you reach the end of a weekend conference or writers retreat during which you snapped photographs all weekend, and suddenly you remember at the end of the event that you have Instagram on your phone? Here is where you can impress your network with a snappy collage of images. *PhotoGrid* is the app that can help you create and prep your collection of images for Instagram.

Launching PhotoGrid, you are given a variety of options: a *Grid* that is a collection of frames ranging from symmetrical to creative, a *PinBoard* that creates a digital bulletin board for you, and *Video Slides* that turn your selected photos into a miniature slide show. (Additional modes, like the *Magazine Cover* option found across the bottom of

PhotoGrid's introduction screen, works only with one photograph.) Once you've designed your collage, PhotoGrid lets you export to Instagram (as well as Facebook, Twitter, Google+, Flickr, and Tumblr). You can compose your message (including hashtags) in PhotoGrid and export your image directly into Instagram for final touches.

Collages are eye-catching and fun to put together. They also tend to bring in more likes and comments.

Vidstitch

PhotoGrid takes your Instagram photos to the next level by creating sharp, slick collages. *Vidstitch* is a step above PhotoGrid because it allows you to incorporate a small video clip into one frame of your collage. With an in-app purchase (Vidstitch is available to buy through Instagram), you can expand your gallery of frames to include widescreen images, allowing for more still shots to accompany your video, or you can upgrade Vidstitch to the Pro version, allowing you to create a collage of videos. The interface and workflows for Vidstitch are a touch more complicated than PhotoGrid; but with a bit of practice, you can create some eye-catching, engaging content for Instagram.

Repost

With the ability to share postings on Facebook, to retweet on Twitter, and to reblog on Tumblr, you would think Instagram would offer this function in its own app, but presently it does not. This is a shame, as some Instagram photos you may come across are nothing less than stunning and others capture a mood that you want to share with your network.

The app Repost allows you to easily share images from other Instagram accounts, working as a retweet function. In the spirit of proper accreditation, Repost watermarks the image with its original Instagram account and populates your Post window with the original accompanying post. You can edit the post, or clear it completely, but the image will always name the originating Instagram account. Repost is a great option for sharing the work of others and providing engaging content of your own.

The app also allows you the ability to like images in your Instagram feed, and even create an index of favorites in case you want to repost or reference another image later. Repost offers account management beyond Instagram's basic functions, making it a must-have in your third-party applications for Instagram.

InstaQuote

This app, of all the third-party apps featured in this chapter, has proven itself to be a fantastic tool for promotion. How? InstaQuote, on a basic level, allows you to make square images with simple, artistic backgrounds, the focus of the art being text of various styles. The GUI gives you two areas to type text, the fields divided by a single line. The larger area, which asks, "What was said?" is where your quote goes, while the smaller area, which asks, "Who said it?" is where you type the source of the quote. Then, by tapping key words in your quote, you can add emphasis by changing the base color of the words.

Upgrading to the pro level not only removes the InstaQuote watermark, but it also imports a wide variety of backgrounds—textures, abstracts, airbrushes—and allows you to import your own photographs for the purpose of creating your own backgrounds. InstaQuote makes pull quotes from blog posts, teasers from your books or works-in-progress, and inspirational quotes that keep you motivated extremely easy to create and post on Instagram, as well as, on Facebook and Twitter.

Iconosquare

While Iconosquare is not available as a mobile application, it's still worth looking at from an analytics perspective. This app offers a deep look into your feed, who you are following, and how other Instagrammers are reacting to your content. Under the *Statistics* menu and the submenu *Rolling Month Details*, analytical data is collected on followers you have picked up, followers who have dropped you, how your most recent post compares to previous ones, and which images are seeing the most engagement. Iconosquare also allows users outside of the Instagram app to fully manage their account. You can like photos from your feed, follow and unfollow other Instagrammers, reply to comments, and even perform a *repost* function similar to the Repost app. All of these are things the Instagram app does not allow you to do. Iconosquare can also post your images on a variety of social media platforms.

BOOKMARK

Iconosquare offers an analytics section called *Tag Impact* under the *Optimization* menu of your account. This is an essential section to watch: Tag Impact tracks all the hashtags you use with your media over a ninety-day period. On the left-hand side you'll find your tags—your most frequent hashtags are larger and in bold. On the right-hand side are the top hashtags used across all of Instagram. If you want traffic and network growth, you will want to find tags that fit your media.

While Iconosquare may look like a one-stop solution, the downside of this website is that it is not portable. At the time of this chapter's publishing, there is no smartphone app for Iconosquare, making it less versatile than the other third-party apps covered here. Still, Iconosquare is an essential tool for success with Instagram.

With so many options and so many capabilities, it is easy to see not only why Instagram is as popular as it is, but also how powerful a platform it can be in conjunction with third-party applications. Instagram has a lot of potential, so take your strategy one step at a time and consider which of its many options will work best for you.

I do love Instagram. The artistic aspect of sharing our general lifestyle through pictures is so easy through the app. So many people are visual. It's a unique outlet for an author.

—DR. STACIA KELLY, HOLISTIC HEALTH COACH
AND AUTHOR OF *REDUCE YOU* AND *SLIM, FIT, HAPPY YOU*

BEST PRACTICES ON INSTAGRAM

When you hear about networking platforms or building a presence on social media, authors generally talk about Facebook, Twitter, and blogging straight away. Sometimes podcasting and Google+ are mentioned.

Instagram?

On our own networks, while writing this chapter, we asked our community of writers what questions they had about Instagram. Writer, podcaster, and photographer J.R. Blackwell said point-blank "Should I even bother?" She went on to say she didn't think Instagram was a bad platform (and as she is a professional photographer, we would have been surprised if she thought it was), but the question was how would it be a good platform for authors?

What a great question.

Instagram is a social media outlet writers in general do not seriously consider a viable promotion platform. They may try it out for a brief spell, have a bit of fun, and then forget they have the app on their smartphone. With the right approach and application, though, Instagram can provide a treasure trove of visual content for a writer. Now, before you think that "visual content" for a writer consists of nothing more than a picture of a laptop with a work-in-progress on the screen (which we've found that followers on Instagram and elsewhere do respond to!), think again. It's possible to cast a more imaginative net by including character inspirations, behind-the-scenes research or travel, or even a quick link back to your blog. You must go beyond a writer's desk or book signings. The key is how you approach your content.

Author Appearances

Book signings can only be so interesting. A snapshot of you with pen at the ready and books arranged neatly is fine, but then what? Depending on the appearance and the location, quite a bit. If you are appearing with other authors on a panel discussion, you can take a photo of the discussion. After the panel, why not snap a candid shot with the other authors or editors attending? (Ask if they are on Instagram so you can tag them accordingly, but make sure you spell their names right!) You can also post Instagrams that document your travel to various conventions and conferences where you will be presenting. Geotag where each of these moments is taking place and invite readers within driving distance to join you there. You can also repost images or video from other authors' feeds to boost the signal, provided you know of other Instagram-using writers who are attending the event with you.

Upcoming Releases, Special Events, and Cover Reveals

Do you have a date for your next novel or approval from your publisher to reveal your next book cover? Instagram allows you to easily share artwork pertaining to your upcoming launch. Whether it is an original graphic cooked up in the image editor or a cropped section of your cover, Instagram—with Iconosquare added into the mix—gives you the ability to send out a single post across seven social networks. This post can point back to one central location, whether it's your blog, a link to pre-order your book, or another place on the Internet. You can also create original artwork publicizing special events—a crowdfunding event, a charity anthology, or an upcoming appearance—where you will be participating. The image you create for Instagram can also serve as your own branded artwork for the event in question.

Crowdfunding is a business model many authors are taking advantage of. Authors ask audiences to invest in a project, namely a book, a series, or other form of media—games, Web series, graphic novels. The investments go toward a final goal that will bring the project to fruition. Of all the various crowdfunding services, *Kickstarter* is the best known. Authors have made the most of Kickstarter's ability to raise money for their works—usually dedicated funds for editing and cover design. In return for the backers' money, they offer "rewards" like print and audio copies of the books, exclusive short stories, or other items that might incentivize people to lay down their money for their project.

Insta-Competitions

Competitions are a proven way to increase your number of followers on Instagram, but don't go this route until you have at least a small following. It's hard to make a splash if only a few people are following you.

Right off the bat, Instagram is nice enough to spell out rules for promotional guidelines. You are responsible for the lawful operation of your contest—this makes sure Instagram isn't in trouble if you fail to obey local laws. You cannot ask your readers to inaccurately tag content or people in their entries. All promotions must have a note from Instagram that releases the company of responsibility, and all entrants must point out that Instagram is not endorsing, sponsoring, or administering the contest. Instagram will not help out with your promotion nor give you any advice pertaining to it. Finally, you must agree that you are running the contest at your own risk. Keep those guidelines in mind while you design your giveaway. User-generated content competitions are popular on Instagram and a great way to encourage creativity among your followers. They also have the advantage of not running afoul of any local laws governing sweepstakes.

In order to fit in all the rules, prizes, and directions for entrants, you should create a post or page on your blog or website. You then put this URL in your Instagram post. The hashtag that you are using to keep track of entrants will be included as well.

So what do you ask people to do? Keep it simple, and make sure it involves nothing dangerous or too outrageous. A picture of a participant with your book ("book selfies"), dressed up like a character, or posing with something significant to the book (an artifact or some related item) are all good choices. Or you could go with something related to your genre that is more open to interpretation.

BOOKMARK

Whether on Instagram or any social network, when hosting competitions, make sure the prize is enticing enough. It doesn't have to be expensive. Advanced Reading Copies make great prizes, or you can offer a selection of items related to your book. Writer Starla Huchton has written books about superheroes and often gives away well-thought-out prize packs of items with superhero themes.

Before launching the competition, make your own competition graphic to post on Instagram, and make sure it is attention grabbing and contains the hashtag you have come up with.

Don't forget to spread the word about your competition via your other social networks.

Teasers and Motivationals

Selections from your upcoming release are always great teases to get readers excited, but in the social media arena, authors need to grab a reader's attention. In the same way graphic designers use pull quotes from a magazine article to grab a reader's attention, authors are now using teasers, juicy character quotes, and small chunks of narrative to tantalize readers with what is to come in their next work. Teasers work here the same way Hollywood entices rabid fans with iconic imagery in a movie poster—you give your readers just a hint of what is coming.

Motivationals are similar to teasers, but they come from your blog. While you might ask, "Isn't it a little arrogant to offer up my writing advice as sharable quotes alongside Stephen King, J.K. Rowling, and Mark Twain?" Consider the motivational you create less of a "Bask in my brilliance!" graphic and more of a "This is what I want you to take away" graphic—a visual representation of a blog post bestowing writerly advice, if you will. On Instagram, motivationals and teasers are terrific promotions for your novels and short stories.

In accompanying posts, links are not active on Instagram, but when posted on Facebook and Tumblr with the *http://* lead-in, URLs can take readers from your cross-posting to wherever you want them to go.

The Writer's Life

Photos of what you're reading, what's on your computer screen, print resources on the corner of your desk, or where you are drawing inspiration from make for interesting visual content. It's a peek behind the curtain, a delightful look at what inspires you and what words are filling the page. Depending on how much you want to share, you can also post the sunrise from a morning walk or your view from a writer's retreat. There's a lot that goes into writing a book—share it on Instagram.

Writers off the Clock

Are you heading out to the movies? Are you hosting a cookout with other creative types? Maybe you're in the conference's hotel bar or restaurant with other authors. Little moments in life can be fun to share with your community. If those in the picture are comfortable sharing these candid memories with your network, do it. Posting your adventures away from your keyboard is a great way to connect.

A lot of writers use Instagram, and you know what? We need an identifying hashtag. So if you are a "storyteller on Instagram" posting a photo about your creative process, a successful appearance, or something that inspires you, be sure to use #stoig. This will show that you are a writer taking advantage of this visual social media platform.

As you can see, there are lots of great ways to crack open the door for your readers or potential readers, and to let them get a visual of what it is like to be a writer.

Next we're going to look at some of the smaller, less well-known platforms that might suit you and your writing. Let's take the path less traveled and see what we can find in the undergrowth.

CHAPTER 10

Additional Options
Platforms that Break the Conventions

The social media space is always evolving, and new platforms are constantly springing up to demand the attention of readers and writers alike.

Some platforms generate wild interest for a few days or weeks before being cast aside; some new ones offer features or conveniences that the old ones do not and are taken into the fold.

Authors should always keep their eyes on the social media horizon to see what is newly available, but before they sign up at any site, they must evaluate it. Does the site offer new audiences? Is it reaching more people than an already established sites? Is there some new aspect of marketing that can be achieved with it that others do not offer? In particular, are readers gathering in this new place?

The platforms we cover here are not as mainstream as Facebook, Twitter, or Instagram, but these are networks that are popular with authors, where writers are found frequently, and where they can sometimes find a new and unique angle to promote their work or just be themselves.

GOODREADS

Around since 2007, Goodreads.com grew into one of the largest gathering spots for readers, which makes the site hard to ignore as a writer. In 2013, Amazon announced it was buying Goodreads, and when the giant of the book business is interested in a corner of the Internet, you should be, too.

In that very same year, the site had twenty million users. Now, that number may be small compared to other social media networks, but those twenty million are all passionate readers, who interact and are committed to book culture. Users log books they have read, or want to read, then review these books, gather in groups to talk about them, and make lists like "best steampunk" or "books with amazing female characters." It's safe to say Goodreads is the world's largest book group.

With all that going on, you might want to jump in with both feet, but here are a few words of caution.

Goodreads can be a great place for authors to connect with readers, but authors should tread carefully. Readers are very protective of their space and do not welcome solicitation in it. Any interaction you have with them must be well thought out.

None of this means that authors should not go into this arena, mind you. You just need to be careful. For example, Lists—a collection of books showcased around a theme like "Essential Fantasy" or "Classic Science Fiction"—that you create do not always belong to you once they go live. When receiving reviews of your titles or titles you are affiliated with, defending your work from readers is not the best course of action. Goodreads does offer ways to promote and interact with readers, however, such as having your blog posts appear in your own profile and offering various giveaway opportunities that they will assist you in planning. If you want to interact with your readers, stick to those outlets.

When it comes to the reviews posted, as we mentioned earlier, it's important to remember one rule: You're not going to please everyone. If

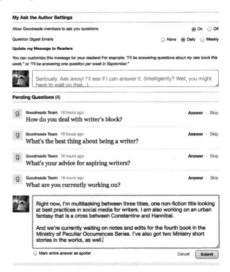

you see any of those dreaded one-star reviews or even reviewers who make personal comments about you, do not engage.

We repeat: *Do not* engage.

Of course there have been cases in which authors and readers have exchanged heated words. Some of them have been fairly managed, but most work their way through other social media networks, becoming cautionary tales shared between authors and would-be professional writers looking for ways to avoid making mistakes in their careers.

Stay on the marked path, and you will have another fine venue to market your book.

Getting Started

Creating a Goodreads account comes first. Make sure you have a good profile, description, and links back to your website. Next, go find yourself on Amazon, Smashwords, BarnesandNoble.com, and elsewhere. If you are published, you are likely on Goodreads, or at least a public profile is linked to your books. Click your name. You are now on your public author profile, different from the profile you created, but not for long.

At the bottom of the page click on "Is this you?" This will result in a request to join the author program. It may take a day or two to be approved, but once you receive the confirmation e-mail, your two profiles will be merged.

In your profile, link back to your blog so newly published posts immediately appear on your Goodreads profile. Then fill in the rest of the details of your writing career.

You can open yourself up to questions, which is a fun way to interact with your readers. Don't forget to add events and your favorite authors.

Goodreads Giveaways

Like the other platforms, giveaways are an excellent way to get your name out to readers. Some restrictions do exist, however. Goodreads has (as of now) decided not to allow e-book giveaways, but we understand they are working behind the scenes with publishers to change that. Presently, giveaways are for print books only.

You can run more than one giveaway. In fact, Goodreads suggests running one before your book becomes available and one after. To get started, check out the Giveaways page. Fill in all the details, then submit it for review. Goodreads runs a tight ship, so it has to clear every giveaway before allowing it out into the wild.

Selling Books on Goodreads

Until about a year ago, Goodreads let authors sell their books directly. However, since Amazon purchased it in 2013, that service went away. Amazon is continuing to integrate its services, and that means Amazon wants you to sell your book through its website. In your author profile settings, under *book links*, you can set the order or hide links to booksellers. When readers visit each individual book page, they will be presented with a set of links so they can buy copies.

REDDIT

Reddit is described as a social networking service where users can submit content which is then voted up or down (in terms of popularity, usefulness, insightfulness, etc.) by a network of users. If you are old enough to remember online bulletin boards, then you are going to be right at home on reddit. Unlike those boards in the 1990s, however, reddit is massive and divided into an impossible-to-count number of *subreddits*—topics any user can create. With so much content, it can feel a little daunting at first.

As an author venturing into reddit, you should stick to the books subreddit at first. This is our familiar area after all. This is a moderated subreddit, so look on the right-hand sidebar to take note of the rules for participating in this community. The books subreddit is one of the most populated places readers can go to discuss books. Forty thousand new subscribers come on board every week. Books even has its own book group, which must be the largest anywhere (outside of Goodreads) at twelve thousand members. Just imagine trying to get that many folks into a room at once.

From this subreddit, you can drill down if you like, but since we are concentrating on the social aspect of these other platforms, let's check out one of the more popular and allowable ways for authors to use reddit.

Ask Me Anything (AMA)

AMAs are quickly becoming the go-to way for authors to spread the word about their books and to connect with readers who may have already read them. AMAs are not restricted to authors—even Barack Obama has done one—but they can be fun and informative. You are basically creating a worldwide chance for readers, both potential and otherwise, to ask you questions.

BOOKMARK

Carefully read over the AMA FAQs[1] to make sure you know the procedure for both requesting an AMA and creating one.

STORIFY

When you first sit before its interface, you may think "This is just another blog engine," but *Storify* is unlike any other blog engine you may come across.

First, Storify wants to help you tell a story, which is why it offers a search engine that scans blogs, Facebook, Twitter, and a host of other social networks in its interface. You can search by user, by keywords, or by a regular search string, and you will get a window of results for whatever social platform you want to tap into.

Storify then offers you the ability to click and drag featured images with opening lines of a blog post, multiple Twitter posts, and updates

---

1 http://www.reddit.com/r/IAmA/wiki/index

from whatever platforms you are searching and feature them in the post you are putting together. The end result is very similar to posts you may see on Mashable, BBC News, CNN, io9, and other news services where instead of simply screen captures, you have captures of the updates that take you to the source material in one click.

Finally, once you have created your Storify post, you can access the HTML code behind this advanced blog post design, copy it, and paste the raw code into your WordPress blog. Doing so brings instant, dynamic content to wherever you send your audience on a regular basis. Storify is a growing trend with authors, good for referencing things that are happening online or on other networks. It provides updates in context to your own thoughts, a once-difficult task accomplished with random URLs and screen captures now made interactive on your own blog.

Twitter moves fast, which means impactful tweets can miss their audience. That's why I love Storify, especially for compiling writing advice. It allows you to capture tweets—both your own and those of other Twitter users—arrange them in the order of your choice, and embed the full package onto your blog, along with comments on the overall theme. Whether you're imparting knowledge, participating in a discussion, or capturing a hashtag, it's a great boon to assemble all those 140-character bursts into a complete story that will endure long after your tweets have fallen off the page.
—DELILAH S. DAWSON, AUTHOR OF THE BLUD SERIES, *SERVANTS OF THE STORM, HIT,* AND *WAKE OF VULTURES* (WRITTEN AS LILA BOWEN)

Storify is a new platform that you, as a writer, should spend some time getting to know. If you like it, you can work it into your platform, especially if posts are inspired by activity on other social networks.

You know, all this talk about social media, its capabilities, and what an author can do with it has certainly left us parched. We could use a drink …

A SOCIAL'S SOCIAL: UNTAPPD, VIVINO, AND DISTILLER

Authors can close deals, create new contacts, and expand leads for future writing gigs just about anywhere, but perhaps the best wheeling-and-dealing happens at the bar. Occasionally dubbed "BarCon," a lot of networking happens in a conference hotel's bar. Social media comes into play when you are off the clock at a convention, expo, or conference. Its innovative ways connect you with other writers, readers, and the world. But

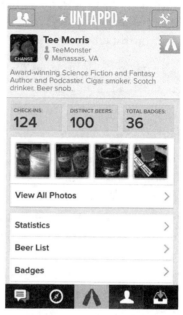

these networks exist simply to provide writers a place to share a frosty beverage or a celebratory round once a contract is signed or a day of book signings are done.

Untappd

Untappd is a network built for those who love beer. Whether you enjoy a porter, a pilsner, or an IPA, Untappd connects you with ice-cold brewskis and the breweries behind them. The network is operated either on a website or a mobile application, and offers you access to Untappd's beer database comprised of mainstream breweries, up-and-coming microbreweries, and home brewers you may meet on your travels. At the core of the app are the reviews. When your first round arrives, you search for your beer in the Search bar across the top. Once you tap your beer from the list of offered brews, you select Check-In and are offered a field where you can:

- Type in a brief review (best at around 150 characters);
- Add a photo of what you are drinking (or who you are drinking with, as we once did with award-winning author Elizabeth Bear);
- Rate your brew;
- Add your location.

But what if beer isn't your thing? That's okay, as Untappd also includes ciders and meads in its database.

Vivino

For wine lovers, *Vivino* is the app of choice. Much like its ale-driven counterpart, Vivino allows you to rate and review wines, but it's how you find a wine in the Vivino network that is particularly clever. Point your camera at the wine bottle's label and take a photo. Vivino will scan its database and find the wine you currently have in front of you, or allow you to enter all of the information about this wine (vineyard, category, vintage, country of origin), along with your own comments. This wine lover's network also scans wine lists, offering reviews and notes about the glasses and bottles featured, price lists for wines you may want to stock your own cellar with, a "location search" that shows you what wines are near you, and your own statistics—what you've tried, what you've liked, and what you didn't.

Now that we have our beer snobs and wine connoisseurs covered, we will turn to an app that would have sparked the interest of rogues and rascals like Ernest Hemingway, Raymond Chandler, and Hunter S. Thompson.

Distiller

Distiller covers scotch, bourbon, rye, and other kinds of whiskey. The app and website grant members access to both trending and recent whiskey rated by the network and the Tasting Table, which is Distiller's own inner circle of experts and enthusiasts who come together to offer recommendations for what you should be enjoying by the fire pit or after dinner. Wish lists can be built alongside your Collection and your Top Shelf, all of which are shared on your profile.

Building Your Brand

These are clever apps, sure, but this book is about social media for writers. How can authors take advantage of these uncommon networks? It's a worthwhile question, as these networks don't necessarily lend themselves to promotion of your books.

Your *brand*, however, is a different matter.

If you visit TeeMorris.com, you will see in the site's title "Unbelievable Beer Snob," a self-proclamation that Tee is proud of. With many check-ins from Untappd, Tee has made his love and appreciation of microbrews a part of his brand.

But when it comes to posting on these networks, authors can add a casual flavor to their social media platforms:

- **INSTANT CONTENT FOR OTHER SOCIAL NETWORKS:** Untappd, Vivino, and Distiller all offer integration with larger networks like Facebook, Twitter, and Google+. With the incorporation of photos, these apps offer your networks dynamic content that can easily spark discussions and other recommendations that you can explore at social events. These platforms can also offer you a new way to connect with potential interests that your readers may have— remember, your readers want to get to know *you*. Untappd, Vivino, and Distiller provide new and varied content to your various platforms, and variety is essential to success.

- **DINING RECOMMENDATIONS FOR YOUR AREA OR AREAS NEW TO YOU:** Whether you want to offer an impromptu meeting place for fans or are looking for a place to try on the road, these barfly apps can automatically access your location to see what people are saying about featured labels—be they local, international, or just new to you. These apps also work as a kind of *Urbanspoon* or *OpenTable* (both apps designed to recommend dining options in your immediate area) for various restaurants, brewpubs, or even vineyards, cideries, and distilleries.

- **GETTING TO KNOW YOUR FELLOW AUTHORS:** We originally met the earlier mentioned (and quoted) Elizabeth Bear at a steampunk event in 2013. But it was 2014 when Tee connected with her on Untappd. Since then, he has shared quite a few toasts and notes with the acclaimed science fiction and fantasy author. Appreciators and aficionados of beer, wine, and spirits love to exchange notes on what they are drinking and where they are drinking it. It's fun to do, and you get to know the tastes of your friends who are dedicated to their literary pursuits. With Distiller's ability to share wish lists across other networks, a bottle of a desired or favorite label makes for a wonderful gift.

BOOKMARK

We already mentioned Ernest Hemingway, Raymond Chandler, and Hunter S. Thompson in the pool of writers who enjoyed a good drink, but it's worthy to note Jean Stafford, Dorothy Parker, and Edna St. Vincent Millay as well. Some of them may have loved their drink a little too much.

You may hear authors joke about BarCon, about partying like rock stars, but not everyone enjoys a good scotch, wine, or beer. If you mention these apps in conversation and authors prefer not to share on any of them, or simply don't drink, you can always get to know them via other channels.

And when offering to buy a round, don't make a big deal if someone chooses an iced tea *not* from Long Island. Respect your fellow authors' choices, and enjoy the social time regardless.

- **SHARING A CELEBRATION OR A QUIET MOMENT WITH FANS:** Readers love to feel a connection with their favorite author. The limits of how much you want to share, as we have said before, are up to you, but fans do appreciate when authors share images of toasts and celebrations. You can be sitting by a fire pit with a single malt in hand or toasting with other authors to a recent award, accomplishment, or appearance—sharing the round through these apps can create a "bonding" moment with your readers.

A dear friend of ours, social media professional Megan Enole, has been known to say, "Never forget the *social* in social media." If these are words to live by (and they are), then the thing that makes these three unique networks so much fun is also the thing that's so good for writers and their platforms—Untappd, Vivino, and Distiller are all about being social. When you want to celebrate, when you want to unwind, or when you want to suggest a favorite drink, why not invite the world to enjoy a round with you? Untappd, Vivino, and Distiller, when used *responsibly,* offer a lot in the way of developing your brand.

TSU.CO

The first thing you need to know about *Tsu* is that this platform is pronounced "Sue." The second thing you need to know is that it still has the new-car smell on it. Tsu only launched in October 2014, but it has already generated a bit of buzz. Comparatively speaking, it is Facebook before it got big and Twitter with more words to work with.

Something that Tsu is doing differently than Facebook is paying its contributors for content. Tsu makes ad revenue, and after keeping 10 percent for operational costs, it pays the rest back to users. It divides users into two pools: one for content creators and one for those who click on the links. Don't get too excited at the moment, since Tsu is still pretty small, but it is something to consider going forward.

Tsu also has developed a vigorous antispam policy in response to its initially being a beacon for spamming in its early days.

There are two kinds of contacts you can have: Friends or Follows. Friends share information with each other, while Follows have only a one-way connection.

Unlike Facebook, which has been throttling down on organic reach, Tsu lets it loose, hence the "before Facebook got big" descriptor. But like Facebook, it does have analytics that will help authors determine which posts are working for them. Advertising on Tsu is still in development stages—if you want to advertise, you have to contact Tsu directly—but that is bound to change in the near future.

So while it is brand-new, authors are already moving into the space. Romance authors, including Piper J. Drake, seem to be the groundbreakers on this fresh social media platform. Along with its main website, Tsu has an app for Android and Apple devices, so you can try it out on the go if you like.

On the Internet not everything succeeds, and Tsu may disappear or it may flourish. It totally depends on how many users it can attract. Tsu is still in its toddler stage, but it sports a clean interface, a shallow learning curve, and some interesting concepts in generating revenue and maintaining a level of quality in shared content. As a writer, you should keep this site in mind as a potential platform. If you have some time to dabble, you might want to consider what it can offer you.

As you can see, there is not a lack of social media for an author to take advantage of. Once again, it is all about finding out where *your* audience is and making yourself available there. Next we're going to explore how to increase your chances of being found online, the thing you really want to achieve with your social media platform. Yes, it's time for us to have that all-important talk about search engine optimization, or SEO.

SEO
Dark Arts of Search Engine Optimization

You cannot work your way through online marketing and public relations without having to contend with three letters that strike terror into the hearts of business owners, Internet novices, and transmedia storytelling professionals everywhere: *search engine optimization* (more commonly known as SEO). If you ask digital-savvy authors, "What is SEO?" you will get a wide variety of answers:

- It's a shell game soaked in snake oil and served on a deed ownership to the Brooklyn Bridge.
- It's essential to success on the Internet; namely, being *found* on the Internet.
- It's magic that's so black it makes Voldemort turn to Darth Vader with arms wide open as he implores, "Hold me closer, Tiny Dancer."
- It's a detail that needs to be seen to in (almost) everything you do in social media.

SEO constitutes all of these things and so much more, and in this chapter you are about to get a crash course in how it works, why it is important, and, more vitally, why you should remain wary of any "foolproof strategy" that guarantees you'll dominate the Top Ten of any search. Before applying the basics of SEO to your social media plan, though, it helps to know why SEO is not the "be all, end all" of social media strategies.

WHY SEO DOESN'T WORK (AS THE "GURUS" CLAIM IT DOES)

If you sense that we are unconvinced of the effectiveness of search engine optimization, it is because we are. We have watched authors invest time and money into self-proclaimed SEO "experts" (who we call "gurus") that convince them that no one will *ever* find them on the vast wasteland of the Internet—unless they hire gurus like themselves to SEO their website.

SEO does matter and it can make a difference—on a somewhat basic level—but there are several reasons behind our skepticism. Our attitude towards SEO comes from information from experts online and elsewhere. We think these experts have disproven this strategy.

The Math Behind SEO Just Doesn't Add Up

Picture a room full of thirty authors, all of whom write science fiction set in a dystopian world where dinosaurs have re-emerged and gasoline is the precious resource that all factions—peaceful and warlike—need in order to survive. These thirty authors have gathered to hear an SEO guru's advice on how to meet their search engine optimization needs. This guru says, "I can guarantee you a place in the top ten list of search results for 'dystopian dinosaur science fiction with gladiator cars' provided you follow my strategy." Sounds great, but remember the head count? There are thirty people in the room, and there are ten slots in that coveted top ten. What if these authors were just science fiction authors? Or what if these authors have books in all genres? Would this expert's strategy still work?

Trying to Read a Reader's Mind Is Impossible

Continuing with this room full of thirty authors and the idea of all of them writing in the same niche (science fiction), the SEO guru claims, "You need to make sure 'dystopian dinosaur science fiction with gladiator cars' is in your meta keywords, descriptions, and content, phrased exactly like that." Why, you ask? "Because that is how Google finds you and how Google will list you in search engine results." So, in theory, if people surfing the Web use "dystopian dinosaur science fiction with gladiator cars," they will see these authors' names in the search results. What happens, though, if the search string is "apocalypse dinosaur sci-fi with modified automobiles" instead? How will the results differ? An aspect of SEO hinges on what keywords people use for a search, and if you select the wrong keywords in a search, there is no guarantee to the end results—and this is for our niche authors. The chances of these people being found on generic searches for "science fiction" and "author" become less and less, even when "science fiction" and "author" are used in meta tags.

Trying to Read Google's Mind Also Helps Your Results

As if reading the minds of Web users who are (supposedly) searching for you at random isn't stressful enough, SEO relies heavily on Google's algorithms, which Google reserves the right to change at any time. *Algorithms* are rules Google sets for search strings to follow and properly display results. Violate any of the algorithms and either your website appears low in the rankings or Google red flags your site as malicious, pushing it even lower in the search rankings.

Why would Google do this?

SEO Can Be Very Easy to Game as a System

While some experts try to remain ethical, many unethical gurus take great delight in beating the system. Whether that means using an abnormally large amount of keywords in meta tags, using keywords in page content that changes the entire flow and voice of the page, or placing keywords in URLs that only yield lengthy and hard-to-remember website pages, gurus go crazy with SEO (and charge you for it). If Google changes algorithms again, the gurus come back with a whole new set of SEO rule benders and overhaul your website with them. And charge you for it. Again.

Organic Search Results Always Yield to Paid Search Results

If you were to go to a search engine—be it Google, Bing, or Yahoo!—and type in the search string "What really happened to the dinosaurs," you would get search results promoting a Christian children's book series (of the same title) written by creationists Ken Ham and Dr. John D. Morris. Even removing the word "really" from the search string brings similar results—an "interpretation" of paleontology topping the search results. Many of the top results are paying for those prime slots, and the price tags for these slots may be well out of your budget.

SEO Does Not Apply to All Social Media Platforms

Google+ and YouTube do take advantage of SEO, but Instagram? Not so much. Twitter? Not really. Facebook? Inconsistently. Podcasts? Not at all. Yes, SEO is essential for your blog when it comes to the meta tags that only search engines and browsers see, and also when it comes to the content featured on your blog, but SEO only goes so far in social media. SEO is important, but nothing to lose sleep over.

BOOKMARK

So where does SEO matter in social media?

- Blogging
- Google+
- YouTube

Notice anything about those three platforms? Two of them are Google owned. If you're blogging with Blogger, then you have a triple play because Google owns that blog engine, as well. While you may not need to concern yourself with SEO on Facebook and Instagram, you will want to think about it for these three platforms, particularly YouTube. Keywords and descriptions play heavily in search results on YouTube, just as they would in a Google search string. SEO also matters with blogging engines, except for Tumblr, where SEO is important only if you crack into templates and apply meta tags.

Google Changes Its Algorithms Often

As mentioned earlier, gurus love trying to beat the system. They still game the system to this day with some truly ridiculous tactics. This is one reason why Google changes its algorithms frequently, and while that does make life difficult for gurus, it also makes life more complicated for the rest of us. We now have to make sure our SEO meets with the new standards. Not knowing what Google will or will not change makes it difficult to gauge how much work is ahead of you once a change occurs. It's back to reading minds, and changes from the mother ship can happen without warning.

Now that you know exactly what SEO is not, and why we are somewhat leery of it, let's talk a bit about how SEO *does* work for you, your website, other social media, and author platforms.

HOW TO MAKE SEO WORK FOR YOU

What this chapter will do is create a basic strategy for you to apply. What we're offering are the nuts and bolts of SEO, setting aside past skepticism and bad experiences we have encountered with gurus.

What you need to know, before we go any further, is exactly what *meta tags* are. Meta tags are keywords and descriptions that appear in the header of your blogs, as well as in your YouTube posts and in the titles you may list on Amazon, Smashwords, and elsewhere, if you are an independent publisher or hybrid author. Many kinds of keywords can be implemented, but for our (writers') purposes, we'll focus on the following:

- **TITLES:** These are the titles of your Web pages, whether for your blog, your website, or both. When people are on your website, the title appears in the browser window or tab, as well as in the Recently Visited drop-down menu.
- **DESCRIPTIONS:** Descriptions are brief summaries of what content is featured on a specific page. You can use the same description for an entire website, but it is advised to make each description original.
- **KEYWORDS:** Keywords are the most common search terms people would likely use to find your site.

Other places where keywords matter include:

- **CONTENT:** The actual videos, images, and text visible to people visiting your website
- **IMAGE FILE NAMES:** Tags given to images you use for blog posts and other online content you are sharing

There is a working theory that optimizing URLs is essential in good SEO, but speaking from past experience, we can tell you that keywords in URLs are useless, and they can inadvertently red flag your site on Google and make it hard for people to find you.

The current trend in SEO is that meta keywords are secondary to meta descriptions in priority. This trend can easily change, however. It is prudent for you, when laying down the groundwork for SEO on your website, to follow these limits:

- **PAGE TITLE:** No more than 70 characters
- **META DESCRIPTION:** No more than 160 characters
- **META KEYWORDS:** No more than ten keyword phrases, separated by commas, all in one set of quotes, not individual terms

With these guidelines, you can start developing your own SEO strategy. So, let's focus on that niche fiction of "dystopian dinosaur science fiction with gladiator cars," which sounds more interesting the more we type it. Let's set up a strategy for the home page of your blog or website under the parameters covered here:

- **PAGE TITLE:** *Dino Demolition | Science Fiction from Tee Morris* (49 characters with spaces)
- **META DESCRIPTION:** *From author Tee Morris comes a new adventure where the Past becomes Present, and the fate of the world comes in Regular or Premium Unleaded.* (140 characters with spaces)
- **META KEYWORDS:** *dystopian, apocalypse, future, road warrior, Jurassic, dinosaur, science fiction, Tee Morris*

With the basics of SEO in place, you can now look deeper into the content of your pages. Are there enough keywords present in your pages' content to catch the eye of search engines everywhere?

Social media is the most effective and cost-efficient way to set your work apart, and it's essential in today's marketplace. Gone are the days of the ivory tower where a writer could hide out. Today's readers want to see, hear, touch, and interact with fans, and they smell "fake" or auto-generated a mile away. Choose a persona, be it spiritual, ironic, comical, artistic, etc., and then generate interesting content and conversations across social media platforms in a way that best expresses your personality and brand.

—TOBY NEAL, AUTHOR OF THE MILLION-COPY-SELLING
LEI CRIME SERIES

THE SEO THAT CAN HURT YOU

Optimizing your Web page, whether with keywords or with content, can truly be an epic undertaking, depending on how much work you want to do. SEO shares a few things in common with a process authors are very familiar with: worldbuilding. You can spend hours, days, or even months worldbuilding for a story or novel, and never type out one word. The same thing can happen with SEO. You can apply keywords every place you can think of and inadvertently destroy your website, if not from the inside, then from the outside. SEO can work against you if you remain oblivious to the following traps that, inexplicably, those gurus still practice today.

Hidden Keywords

With some CSS coding, you can actually place images on top of bodies of text. With some extra coding you can easily make a small paragraph of keywords blend into the background and then hide the "blank" space by placing an image over it. This sleight-of-hand is an instant red flag from search engines and can penalize search results for your website.

Stuffing

When we talk about SEO, those new to the Internet usually ask, "Why don't I just load up my keywords tag with a text version of my book?" (No, really, we get asked that.) This is an example of *stuffing*, which is exactly what it sounds like: attempting to come up with every permutation of what people would enter into a search engine. Instead of your keywords looking like this:

> dystopian, apocalypse, future, road warriors, Jurassic, dinosaur, science fiction, Tee Morris

Stuffing turns your keywords into this:

> dystopian, distopian, apocalypse, future, road warriors, road, warriors, Jurassic, dinosaur, dinos, Tyrannosaurus Rex, T-Rex, science, fiction, science fiction, speculative fiction, spec fic, sci fi, specfic, sci-fi, Tee Morris, Tee, Morris

Avoid stuffing in your titles, headings, descriptions, and page content. Not only does this tactic not make any difference whatsoever, search engines regard this as characteristics of spam-related sites.

Forcing Keywords

This is a variation on stuffing, one that deals more with your content and how keywords can affect your posts or pages. Forcing keywords where they do not belong contextually cannot only be risky in how search engines regard your page, but they also can alter the voice of your content. For example, let's say you write up a summary of your genre-mashing novel for your blog's About page:

> From the ashes of society, a hero rises. Mac McKlintock is a loner, driving the highways of a post-apocalyptic world where dinosaurs walk amongst humans. Both prehistoric creatures and survivors of civilization's fall hunt. They hunt for the weak. They hunt for the frightened. For Mac, he survives, and stands for those too tired to fight.

Now, let's say a guru claims to be able to make this summary SEO ready. The guru comes back with your summary looking like this:

> From apocalyptic ashes, a hero rises. Mac McKlintock is a lone road warrior, cruising the desolate highways of the apocalypse, a new Jurassic world where science has brought dinosaurs back from extinction to walk amongst the human survivors. Both prehistoric dinosaurs and what is left of civilization hunt. They hunt for weak humans. They hunt for frightened humans. For Mac, he survives, and in this science fiction adventure he stands for those too tired to fight.

See how stilted, not to mention redundant, the second description is? Ranking high in Google search strings does not necessarily mean more keywords everywhere, but more keywords with *relevance, reputation,* and *popularity.* SEO should not dramatically change the voice of your website.

You can also force keywords into URLs. We have seen for example, simple URLs like this:

> http://ministryofpeculiaroccurrences.com/what-is-steampunk/

... turned into URLs "optimized" for search engines:

> http://ministryofpeculiaroccurrences.com/novels/series/genre/science_fiction/what_is_steampunk_explained_by_author_Tee_Morris.html

Sound ridiculous? Look ridiculous? Guess what? It *is* ridiculous.

When you try too hard in SEO, it does nothing to improve your analytics. Instead, it frustrates people who want to find you quickly and easily online, and more than likely alerts search engines about questionable activity. There is no reason to force square pegs into round holes when working with SEO. Keep it simple, keep it clean, and take advantage of the basics that SEO offers you.

BEST PRACTICES OF SEO

Over the years, SEO gurus have made the skill and art of search engine optimization this murky, mysterious approach to online marketing. SEO does not have to be like this. Much of what is needed to achieve success involves intelligent, educated application of keywords in your website's meta tags and content. There are also plenty of free tools available to keep you in the know, especially if there are any sudden changes in Google's algorithms.

Use Google Keyword Planner

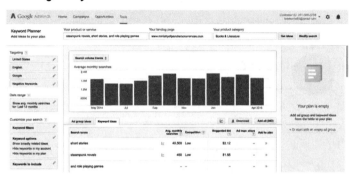

Part of the Google AdWords tool, the *Keyword Planner* provides a user-friendly ability to consult the almighty search oracle Google and get an idea—based on the parameters of your product and services—of the most popular keywords used in search strings. You can then take the keywords generated, export them into a spreadsheet, and begin narrowing down the terms you want to use and apply throughout your website.

Use Google Webmaster Tools

This collection of online resources from Google can help you understand how optimized your website is. Offering in-depth looks at your site's *search traffic*, keywords and pages documented by *Google Index*, and additional statistics, along with possible errors from *Crawl*, the *Webmaster Tools* dive into your website's analytics and performance. Here Google lets you know what keywords are showing up in your content most often, along with variants and relevance to your site. Webmaster Tools also tracks what search strings people are using to find you. Using the Keyword Planner and Webmaster Tools together can help you optimize your website easily.

Write Your Meta Descriptions with Cliffhangers

When writing up meta descriptions, cliffhangers are a clever and enticing approach to encourage viewers to click through. Instead of the original description for our dino-dystopian adventure that currently reads:

> From author Tee Morris comes a new adventure where the Past becomes Present, and the fate of the world comes in Regular or Premium Unleaded.

… we could make the decription more enticing:

> In a future where Past becomes Present, will lone survivor Mac McKlintock remain standing when facing impossible odds, a pack of T-Rexes, and half a tank of gas?

You want to give people a reason to click through to your site, so invite them to enter your world.

BOOKMARK

When encouraging click-throughs with cliffhangers, you should avoid phrases like "Click here" or "Find out more …," as these are associated with link farms and other spam sites. Be creative in your meta descriptions without being obvious.

Use Meta Keywords That Are Original to Your Site

In developing your keywords, you should create them with one question in mind: "Would I follow this link?" Your tags—descriptions, titles, and so on—should invite and beckon others to follow your URL.

This might mean rewriting descriptions and content, and reorganizing the order of your keywords. The keywords and content you develop for your website should be unique to you but not unique to each other.

What follows are two examples of meta descriptions and content from the home page. The first pair shows what not to do. The second is the keeper.

Bad

META DESCRIPTION: In a future where Past becomes Present, will lone survivor Mac McKlintock remain standing when facing impossible odds, a pack of T-Rexes, and half a tank of gas?

FROM THE HOME PAGE: In a future where Past becomes Present, Mac McKlintock is a lone survivor, driving the highways of a post-apocalyptic world where dinosaurs walk amongst humans. Both pre-historic creatures and survivors of civilization's fall hunt. They hunt for the weak. They hunt for the frightened. For Mac, he survives, and stands for those too tired to fight, but what are Mac's chances when facing impossible odds, a pack of T-Rexes, and half a tank of gas?

Good

META DESCRIPTION: In a future where Past becomes Present, will lone survivor Mac McKlintock remain standing when facing impossible odds, a pack of T-Rexes, and half a tank of gas?

FROM THE HOME PAGE: From the ashes of society, a hero rises. Mac McKlintock is a loner, driving the highways of a post-apocalyptic world where dinosaurs walk amongst humans. Both prehistoric creatures and survivors of civilization's fall hunt. They hunt for the weak. They hunt for the frightened. But for Mac, he takes a stand for those too tired to fight.

You want your keywords and content to not only be unique to your work, but also to work together. When keywords and content work independently of one another, search rankings are affected. Your keywords should be the answer to the question people are asking online.

We have been spending a lot of time on Google. The reason, of course, is that Google remains the most accessed of all search engines. Google, at the time of this writing, gives priority to meta descriptions and uses them in search results snippets, provided keywords appear in them. Microsoft's Google-challenger, Bing, follows similar algorithms but does not pay close attention to keywords in the meta description if they are not within the content. (This affects the site's relevance in Bing's search results.) Yahoo! pays close attention to meta descriptions, more so than Google or Bing.

Keep Track of News on Google

Google continues to keep algorithms in flux.[1] We have gurus to thank for this. The real question is how do we keep up with these changes?

- Google's Webmaster Central[2]
- HubSpot[3]
- Moz[4]

Usually when big news occurs back at the mother ship of search engines, other major news outlets like CNN, *Wired*, and *Computerworld* will cover the changes, but the three sources above tend to be reporting both big and small changes, and reporting them faster. While "keywords no longer matter, but descriptions are better" may not seem like a big change to the mainstream media resources, details like this can dramatically affect your site's rankings. When you can, make time for these online resources, as they can keep you ahead of the curve.

---

1 http://blog.hubspot.com/marketing/google-algorithm-visual-history-infographic

2 http://googlewebmastercentral.blogspot.com

3 http://blog.hubspot.com

4 https://moz.com/blog

Search engine optimization carries a lot of baggage with it, but SEO can make a difference in where your website lands in search results, as well as in how people will find you. Reviewing your website's pages for proper SEO is a good idea, but keep it simple. With any strategy to improve your online presence, you can go too deep and begin to litter your website with ridiculous redundancy, or completely alter the tone and voice of your site to where it just sounds odd. Search engine optimization is important, but it should not come at the cost of quality content or clarity in voice. Practice wisely.

Now with the tools in reach, your social media platform needs your attention. However, without developing a voice and providing your networks with content, there is no platform to develop. After all, you want to give people a reason to stick around. Sure, your works are interesting, but they can remain so only for so long before people wander off to another corner of the Internet. You want your website, your platforms, and your voice to be more than just a voice for your work. You want your corner of the Internet to be a one-stop location for news on your work, on your genre, and on works that are related to your genre.

There is no hard-and-fast rule that you have to share everything. In fact, there are no hard-and-fast rules in social media, but there is a need for content. And content is king. Without it, there is no online success. You want to be a voice and a positive, reliable resource for what you write, your genre, your interests, and your industry. Focus on developing the strongest voice possible, and your networks will provide you and your work the strongest of support.

Welcome to the wonderful world of content marketing, where people come to you to stay in the know.

Content Marketing
Promoting with and Through Others

Logic would tell you that investing in some kind of online advertising, whether you pay to show up on other blogs, boost Pages and posts on Facebook, or engage with other social media platforms, would be the easiest way to get the word out about you and your books. This is traditional marking at its core: Pay for the platform in order to reach your audience. This is how marketing has worked since its inception, and if you hear the story behind those who inspired the TV show *Mad Men*, you'll find that marketing is a funny and slightly sneaky business of manipulation, public relations, and showmanship. You have to convince your audience, be they loyal fans or potential readers, that *your book* is *the book* to read, that your series is the next big thing, and that you are a writer to watch. This is how marketing works and has worked for decades.

Follow that same logic with social media, though, and you are more likely to win the lottery than to propel your book up the rankings of Amazon and the bestseller lists at *The New York Times*.

Social media, and those who have mastered it, never forget what is at its core: real people. So many authors forget the *social* aspect of social media. You need to make a connection with your audience and establish yourself not only as a skilled storyteller but also as an expert on what you are writing about. You need to establish trust with your audience, which, to an extent, traditional marketing does, but what traditional marketing fails to understand is that social media is not for bombarding an audience with the same message over and over again (as we have seen numerous times with authors on Twitter saying some version of "Buy my book. It's awesome!" in their feed). Doing so simply drives a social media audience away.

You might notice that those same authors who continuously promote their books have an astounding number of followers—some even reach the tens of thousands. Experience has shown us that most of those followers are purchased. Again, it's a sign of traditional marketing mishandling social media, as it's all about the numbers in traditional marketing.

Marketing and social media, though, have found a happy medium, and there is a good possibility that you have been practicing it already, provided you are online trying out the different platforms. *Content marketing* takes a very different approach in that it promotes through the content of others. In a sense, you are promoting your own works by showcasing someone else's related work.

Perhaps now you may be thinking "Wait a minute. I'm promoting myself by promoting others? That doesn't make sense!" Content marketing follows a different strategy. Instead of your platform centering only on your book, it centers on your interests.

On our own Ministry of Peculiar Occurrences Facebook Page, we feature links about our books, special events where we will be appearing, and links to our newsletter. Our Page (as well as our other platforms like Twitter, Tumblr, and Instagram) also offers news on those who write for *Tales from the Archives*, promotes other steampunk events across the country and around the world, and shares links about steampunk music, fashion, and entertainment. We even feature other authors and their works, especially if the authors are part of our *Tales from the Archives* podcast.

This may seem backwards, especially when we promote other authors' books, but in content marketing you are establishing your blog and your social networks as reliable resources for your subject matter. In the case of the Ministry of Peculiar Occurrences, our expertise is steampunk. What kind of content do our various platforms cover?

- Steampunk
- Dieselpunk
- Atompunk (sometimes called retropunk)
- Victorian history
- Science fiction, fantasy, and horror

That covers a lot of ground when you think about it, but one of the challenges (and joys) of content marketing is asking, "What can I talk about with authority?" Our One-Stop Writer Shop platforms include:

- Publishing news
- Self-publishing news
- Writing tips
- Self-publishing tips
- Marketing and promotion tips

It is incredible how many different topics can directly tie in with your work.

Content marketing allows you to find other voices in your profession who share your interest. You can then share with your readers, fans, and fellow writers terrific resources that inspire you to work harder and write better. You will want to read and research whatever you share or syndicate on your website to be sure the article you're sharing is coming from a credible, reliable source. We consider the "work" in content marketing to be making sure we stand by the resources we share. That may take some time reviewing what's out there, but when you see traffic coming to your blog or your Google+ page, it is a rewarding sight indeed. You're establishing trust with your audience and building a reputation as a reliable resource in a shared interest.

HOW DOES PROMOTING OTHERS REALLY WORK FOR YOU?

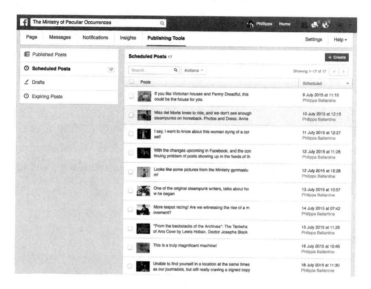

How exactly content marketing works as a promotion tool is still difficult for some authors to grasp. Traditional marketing is all about repetition. It becomes a bombardment of advertising, and an increase in
Twitter followers is perceived as successful. But is it? Are people interacting with you on your networks? Are you talking with your virtual
street team, or are you merely broadcasting the same message over
and over again, eventually turning your signal into noise?

With content marketing, you establish your name and your works
as part of a larger brand, and your website is *the place online* to get
the latest news on your interests. Content marketing begins when you
discover an article that speaks to you and you know sharing it would
resonate with your audience. Once you share it, your audience receives
new content. In turn, the origin of the resource—maybe a blog like Boing Boing, a DeviantArt Web page, or the Instagram of an author like
Piper J. Drake or Bill Blume—receives traffic from your audience. This
sharing benefits both sides, and the person receiving the new traffic,
if savvy, will drive traffic to you in return. This reciprocal approach

SOCIAL MEDIA FOR WRITERS

to marketing builds audiences and communities; the more you share, the stronger your reputation within these circles.

A great example of content marketing at work is Tor.com. A science fiction publisher, Tor delves into far more than just books and its latest releases. Tor.com features columns from authors (even those outside of its catalog) talking about the genre, writing, and media of past and present. The blog also has sections dedicated to upcoming special events (including conventions and expos), art from content creators of all backgrounds, and various discussion threads by readers and writers from around the world. Tor.com has established itself as a go-to resource for relevant content in science fiction, fantasy, and horror, all the while promoting its own brand.

BOOKMARK

We talk a bit about *attribution* throughout the book and in more detail in the Best Practices chapter, but considering how many people completely forget (or ignore) this little detail, it bears repeating: Just because you find something on the Internet doesn't mean it's yours. If you see a post—be it from another author or just a friend—don't turn it into a shareable meme and claim it for yourself. We once caught an author duplicating another's video content, nearly shot for shot. You're a writer and more than capable of coming up with your own ideas. When someone provides content relevant to you (and your audience), make sure you give credit where it is due. A lack of attribution only hurts your online reputation. Avoid violating this rule at all costs.

WHAT CONTENT TO LOOK FOR IN CONTENT MARKETING

When heading out into the wide expanse of the Internet for content, it is a real challenge to find exactly what you are looking for. What is content that makes you think "Oh yeah, this would be great for my audience!" It may sound easy—just find some good articles on a blog here or a Facebook Page there—but you actually need a strategy if you want to provide the best content for your audience.

Reliable Sources

You've heard it said again and again, but before you repost anything, it is always a good idea to dig deep into a Web page, blog, or social media link. Resources like Tor.com, io9.com, *The Washington Post, Mashable*, and *Huffington Post* tend to be rock solid in their research and reliability (but no, they are not perfect). It's when you go to personal blogs or websites that you'll need verification, particularly if you're not familiar with them. You really want to be certain that the news and commentary offered is something that you can stand behind and say, "Yes, I agree." Take a moment to check the resources you're not acquainted with and assure that proper attribution is given.

Current Sources

Try to syndicate and share advice and tips that are relevant. Think of how much publishing has changed over the past five years alone. How relevant would advice on formatting books for e-readers be right now if it was published in 2010 or earlier? Tech news, in particular, has an extremely limited shelf life. You want to find stories, advice, and reviews that date back no more than a year or two, unless it is ever-green content or content that shows "how some things never change" (or "how things have changed since …"). The more up-to-date your resources, the more relevant your site or platform becomes.

Creative Sources

The content you can share, be it your own or content from another source, should stimulate or motivate your creativity. Inspirational quotes or nuggets of advice that inspire you would also make for great content to share. If you are sharing another resource, check its origin just to be sure it is not a site that promotes ideas or agendas contrary to your own. You will also want to check the validity of quotes.

Sometimes quotes are paraphrased or can't clearly be attributed to one person. Sharing comical images, such as memes, can be great for your Web traffic.

Appropriate Sources

This tip tends to be rather tricky to define because everyone's idea of what is appropriate is different. If you are engaging in content marketing for edgy or sensational titles, then your content may reflect that. You define "appropriate" content for your blog or site, but remember the content you share reflects you, your brand, and your titles. There is no consistency between when readers "give a pass" to authors and their opinions and when readers hold authors accountable. Therefore, when you post content outside of your brand, your series, or your title, and that content expresses political, religious, sensitive, or edgy humor or topics, keep in mind that the content reflects on you—possibly in ways that you may not like. Set boundaries for yourself, and remember that your boundaries may still be out of bounds for some. Be ready to face pushback if you stray out of your brand's comfort zone.

When working with content marketing, you will want to be patient and consistent. There is no magic bullet, no surefire formula, and no foolproof way to gain traction overnight, so you have to find a schedule and a pattern, and stick with it in order to build your platform.

Figuring out what works with your audience can be frustrating. Sometimes it will be the post about your book that will result in traffic and numbers, and sometimes a post from another source that caught your eye will drive traffic. What matters in the end is the quality of your content. If you provide your Page, your Instagram, or your blog followers with quality content, and you turn your platform into a go-to source for reliable resources and fantastic media, you will establish a connection between you, your audience, and your work. When you've established yourself as an authority on a topic, people will find your work.

WHEN CONTENT MARKETING GOES BAD

Content marketing can be a positive, community-building strategy for any business, whether you're a writer, editor, publisher, or even a literary agent. However, some writers and social media mavericks regard any online content as free for use, free of responsibility or credit. This unethical approach to sharing content, as we have mentioned before, is known as *scraping*. Similar to when blog content is syndicated without attribution, scraping occurs when the origins of the content are removed and posters tag the accompanying content with their own page, giving the appearance that the shared content is original.

Another dark side of content marketing is establishing a social media platform with only one goal: collecting thousands upon thousands of Likes, Favorites, and other statistics in order to eventually sell the account to the highest bidder. Along with scraping content, the following is a list of ways some of these bogus accounts collect massive numbers:

- Meme generation
- Quizzes
- Photographs and artwork (posted without attribution)
- "Follow-for-follow" campaigns

Social networks attempt to crack down on these unethical accounts, usually through the diligence of their users. Keeping tabs on billions of users, however, can be a daunting task. When putting together your brand's platform, strategy remains key in a successful social media campaign, but it is good to remain aware of what bad content marketing looks like. It is easy to lose yourself in social media's numbers game, and while it may appear that these questionable tactics work in building up your following, quality should always trump quantity. Aim to provide essential, relevant content that will bring people to your Page and keep them coming back, and you will make a strong support system of your platform.

Content marketing that's carried out with the right strategy and execution can prove to be a better way of promoting your book. By building your brand around a community comprised of more than just readers, you have the potential to build a network of artists, musicians, and other writers, all of whom offer their own platforms as sources of promotion. Be patient and consistent, and make sure you use all of your networks to build a community around your quality content.

CHAPTER 13

Best Practices in Social Media

Social media, in the past decade, has evolved into this great machine of communication and innovation. Today it's hard to envision a business or an individual without some sort of social networking strategy, but in the early days of Facebook and Twitter, it was hard to imagine people conducting business and promotion using social networking. Those skeptical of social media platforms regard them as something their teenage cousins do or stuff they tell their kids not to do at the dinner table. Skeptics view social media as hardly worth serious time and attention.

Perhaps this lack of respect for social media is why so many social media plans fail. Sure, teenagers and twenty-somethings use social media. However, they also wield credit cards, use the Internet, and drive cars. Does this mean we shouldn't take credit cards, the Internet, or cars seriously? Of course not, and yet the mistakes people make in social media can be easily avoided if they take social media—and its potential—seriously.

Here's something to keep in mind when approaching social media: Everything shared between these various networks has *potential*. There is no easy way to handle promotion of any kind, and that includes this brave new world of social media. The self-proclaimed social media "gurus," who claim they know the secret of this new media, which they hope to sell to you for a pretty penny, are the reason this frontier is so hard to cross. We are writers who actively practice and promote social media, and we want to pass along to you an honest, practical look at it.

The only "sure things" in social media are hard work, respect, and knowledge of the medium, and that you need to have a solid, strategic plan if you want to achieve success.

CREATE AN EDITORIAL CALENDAR

Remember: Content is king. From the early days of the Internet to today, this remains true. People want quality content from a blog, a podcast, or a social network.

However, content must be in partnership with *consistency*. There needs to be a rhythm or set schedule to your online updates. A writer cannot simply slap content—even good content—on his blog, Facebook, or elsewhere, and then walk away from it for months on end. One or two, or even a smattering of posts of excellent content will not make much of a splash if they don't come at regular intervals that the consumer can rely on. It's about consistency in posting.

Set a schedule for specific days or post frequently. The best way to manage all of your content, whether blogging, Facebook posting, tweeting, or anything in between, is to set up an editorial calendar that lists when and where you will be posting new content.

Your calendar should list topics or reoccurring columns you are posting on your blog, as well as where you are posting and on which days. For example, your calendar should show that you're posting on blogs and Facebook on Mondays and Wednesdays, while Tuesday and Friday are dedicated to Twitter and Pinterest. Once you have a realistic editorial calendar set up, make sure you stick with it and fulfill the schedule. Map out how many posts will be original content that markets your work, and how many will be informational content.

But don't become a slave to your original plan. Your schedule shouldn't be forever set in stone. Allow your editorial calendar flexibility for when fresh topics and news crop up. You want to be able to take advantage of them, not necessarily for the sake of traffic (although some people do that), but for when you really have something to say about a current topic or trend. People will be looking for keywords, so make SEO work for you by keeping up on what is going on in publishing, writing, and your area of expertise.

Content managed in an organized fashion is much less intimidating for an author than a slapdash approach. With a proper editorial calendar and different outlets featuring daily postings, it will soon become habit rather than a rushed afterthought.

THINK BEFORE YOU POST

When you build a platform in social media, you are building a brand. Your brand reflects what you produce, broadcasting your reliability as an author to your audience. It takes a long time to create a solid brand, but just one ill-thought-out blog post, one impulsive tweet, or one snarky caption on Pinterest can inflict a lot of damage. Snarky statements and other attempts at comedy can backfire in a big way, so it is a good idea to look over an update before it goes live and try to see it objectively. Ask yourself, "Could this be taken the wrong way?" If you aren't sure, then the chances are it could be, but that doesn't mean you shouldn't post it. Just mentally prepare for any blowback. Comedy can be hard on social media.

What is not difficult to find, on the other hand, is controversy. You may be impassioned by something in the headlines, an exchange on Twitter, or an image on Instagram, but before you let your passionate support for a cause fly, ask yourself, "Is this argument worth undertaking?" Do you really understand both sides of the debate? Is the time you spend replying and addressing opposing viewpoints affordable? Or are you on a deadline and want to stay focused? If you do step in the middle of a heated debate, are you prepared to face a negative reaction?

BOOKMARK

You may have heard the term thrown around, but what exactly is a *troll* on the Internet? Not far from their literary counterparts who lurk under bridges to snatch travelers unexpectedly, trolls lurk in the darkest corners of the Internet either looking for arguments to kick up or insults to let fly. Trolls care very little about making a point on either side of an argument. They care more about how much they can rattle people, especially the host of a blog, podcast, or platform. This means the insults can go from juvenile to sensational to deeply personal.

Remember that you have the final say for who says what on your platform. Make sure to take advantage of blocking features, and above all—*don't feed the trolls*. There is a reason you have block functions in many of the social networking tools covered in this book. The best way to handle a troll: block, and walk away.

In fact, any time you look at a post that you've written, stop and ask yourself, "Would I be okay sharing this with a roomful of strangers?" Even though your network comprises friends or followers, the truth is your network does not know you as well as you think. Consider consequences with any update you are about to make before it becomes necessary to break glass and push the red button in case of emergencies.

Finding the Positive

Going along with thinking before posting, here's another good rule before hitting send: Be *positive*.

As a professional using social media, you really don't have the luxury of being able to whine, complain, or go on rants. (Granted the *occasional* rant can be fun, depending on the topic. Pip got good traction on her blog when she raved tongue-in-cheek on the trend in book covers that had lead characters with their heads cropped out.) Many authors have built a community around their reinforcing, positive message, be it in writing advice or lessons learned while on the road with their books. People have enough cynicism and negativity in their regular lives. They may not want to hear it from authors—especially ones they want to enjoy the company of social media with.

So focus on lessons learned and what you want to share. Be charming, funny, witty, and caring. Such qualities will take you far with readers.

Do social media because you like it, not because it's some kind of obligation. Nobody wants to read the blog of someone who is being forced to do it. Just like we don't want to read a book written by someone who hated writing it. Tweet because Twitter is fun for you, not because it's on your checklist. Social media is a great place to meet other people doing what you want to do, and it's also a great place to talk to your audience. Note I said *talk to*, not *yell at*.

You know how we use the phrase "In Real Life" (IRL) to differentiate between what's happening in reality and what's happening on the Internet and on social media? Newsflash: Social media is reality. It's not illusion. We need to treat what happens online like it's real because it is. It's not *A Game of Thrones*. And when you're online, the same rules apply as when you're off-line:

Be awesome.

—CHUCK WENDIG, AUTHOR OF THE MIRIAM BLACK TRILOGY, THE HEARTLAND TRILOGY, AND *ZEROES*, AND HOST OF THE TERRIBLEMINDS.COM BLOG

PARTICIPATE IN BLOG TOURS

These are events that, if managed properly, can be a fantastic way to introduce your words to new readers and, in a reciprocal manner, introduce new bloggers to your readership. These events also give you a good backlist of evergreen content. Blog posts such as these can be easily overhauled, updated, and then repurposed for your own blog. If you are repurposing blog posts, you should wait roughly six months in order to give the original column some exclusivity where it first appeared. It's the friendliest thing to do to maintain good relationships with other bloggers.

The way blog tours work is that you appear as a guest blogger across a network of blogs—blogs that cover a variety of topics or perhaps share a common theme. Other bloggers, once or twice a week, in turn, appear on your blog, sharing topics they would like to cover or ones you have previously suggested. To make tours a success for everyone involved, the content bloggers deliver to one another should be:

- original
- unique from blog to blog
- fall within 500 to 1,000 words

Some bloggers may fail to promptly post others' contributions, but if all participants contribute on schedule, your evergreen content will grow substantially. This gives you many options for posts that can later be repurposed for your own blog or for future guest postings.

BOOKMARK

When you are on a blog tour, you are expected to generate original posts for each stop. Do not create one blog post and offer it as your sole contribution. When embarking on a blog tour, you are committing to your tour hosts new, original, unique content. Make sure you meet that commitment.

CREATE *QUALITY* CONTENT

Content can come from a variety of sources, but your content should always be quality. What defines quality content? It's subjective, but quality content should be clear, concise, edited, and well researched. There is a popular opinion that posting content for content's sake is what matters, not the actual worth of your content, but all of your posts are important because they are a reflection of your work.

So what do people look for in quality content?

Timeliness

When news pertaining to your business hits the headlines, you have roughly twenty-four to forty-eight hours to write, edit, and deliver a blog post. At the latest, you have within a week (roughly five days) to blog your own commentary on a topic. At the time of breaking news, people are specifically searching out articles and angles on this topic. By tapping into the timeliness of a news story, you increase your chances of other blogs picking up and syndicating your blog post. Wait too long, and the opportunity to take advantage of the story and drive traffic will be lost.

Cross Promotion

Once a blog post goes live, Facebook and Twitter should be the beginning of your promotion. While there are automated posting tools like the WordPress plug-in Social that broadcast updates on your blog, these postings feel rather cold. Following a flowchart (similar to the editorial calendar), you should compose an original, accompanying post or tweet and then add it to your latest blog post. This lets your various networks know that while there is crossover between your channels, you are handling each account and keeping content fresh.

Cross-Referencing

Remember that your words reflect directly on you, so it is a good idea to link your references back to your blog posts. Sharing resources and linking back to them is a terrific discussion starter, as commenters will ask more about the sources or spark debates on the resources cited. Sharing links may also encourage traffic to your own website, depending on the generosity and the respect of the referred website. Either way, cross-referencing is a terrific tactic for generating traffic around your blog.

BE VISUAL WHEN POSSIBLE

Nothing attracts attention like a good image. Users consistently interact with images more than text-only posts, across all platforms. Some platforms are particularly focused on images—Pinterest and Tumblr—but posts and tweets will get more eyeballs on your content with the addition of an image. Don't forget: Images in blog posts rule!

Using other people's images can backfire on you, however. Sure, when you are just operating as a social media individual, you might enjoy posting Tom Hiddleston memes, but as a professional trying to keep a good online reputation, you should think twice about it.

And don't forget—as we have mentioned in earlier chapters—that stealing another's meme and slapping your website URL on it is definitely out. Similar to when blog content is syndicated without attribution, "scraping" occurs when the origins of the content are removed and posters tag the accompanying content with their own page, giving the appearance that the shared content is their original content. Turning someone else's content into your own can come back to haunt you.

The safest thing to do when creating your own image is to stick to one you took yourself, or you can find stock photography at sites like depositphotos.com. For a small investment, you will be on safe ground to use these photos, and if you are making your own cover, you can repurpose stock images for that, too.

BOOKMARK

Don't forget to tweak the images for different platforms. Remember, tall images work great on Pinterest and Tumblr. Square ones work best for Instagram and Twitter.

A NEW USE FOR THE POUND SYMBOL: HASHTAGS

Twitter was the first social media platform to take advantage of this feature, but now Instagram, Facebook, and even Pinterest are all tapping into the SEO and trending capabilities of hashtags.

Hashtags (#) are tracking tools that allow you to identify updates and postings under a quick-to-find category in any search engine or platform-specific search. The hashtag first appeared on Twitter on August 23, 2007, when Chris Messina tweeted "How do you feel about using # (pound) for groups. As in #barcamp [msg]?"

Yes, the first update to use a hashtag *was about hashtags*.

Hashtags can be used in a variety of ways, ranging from emphasizing a mood to commemorating a special event to stating a punch line in a joke. For authors, hashtags are best employed in the following ways:

- **WHEN DEVELOPING A NEW TITLE OR PROJECT:** *#amwriting, #amediting, #WIP, #teaser*
- **WHEN WORKING WITHIN A GENRE:** *#steampunk, #UF, #YAFantasy*
- **WITH TWEETS PERTAINING TO A BOOK OR SERIES:** *#MoPO, #LondonUndead, #Redshirts*
- **WHEN IDENTIFYING PROMOTIONS OR DIGITAL APPEARANCES:** *#blogtour, #podcast, #interview*
- **AT SPECIAL EVENTS, LIKE BOOK FESTIVALS AND CONFERENCES:** *#BEA2015, #balticon*

Hashtags are the best way to track discussions and trending topics across a social media platform; you'll even hear opinions from people you are not following. Whether you are using tracking options offered through the official Twitter app, reviewing all Instagram images using a tag, or clicking a tag in a Facebook or Google+ update, hashtags allow you to follow or join in a conversation, provided participants consistently use the same hashtag in conversations and posts.

Not all posts need hashtags, but there are times, current events, and special moments when hashtags are essential.

Book Events and Engagements

When attending book festivals, it is always a good idea to use a hashtag for people to track you and other authors attending the event. Before arriving, try to find out if the event has an official hashtag (most events should have one as they will want metrics to show potential sponsors for the following year's event) and encourage your fellow authors and your network to use it. When creating an official hashtag, keep it easy to remember and as short as possible. For example, the official hashtag for the "HallowRead" event of 2014 wasn't #HallowRead or #Hallow-Read2014, but #HR2014.

Topics of Discussion

If you are composing updates on Instagram, Facebook, or Google+, you can turn key words in your update into hashtags, making your status easily found in a hashtag search. So if you are talking about "a new steampunk short story" you have just written, you should post the status as "a new #steampunk short story" instead. Why use *steampunk* as your hashtag? Steampunk is the term or topic of discussion you want people to find you under. Find those keywords—no more than five, at the most—and let them work for you.

Twitter Chats

There are several writing chats happening on Twitter. As of the writing of this book you can find:

- **#SCIFICHAT:** Sometimes featuring special guests, this weekly chat covers topics of writing science fiction, fantasy, and horror. Hosted by @DavidRozansky and @scifichat on Fridays, 2–4 P.M. EST
- **#YALITCHAT:** This chat doubles as a celebration and networking opportunity for readers and writers of young adult fiction. Hosted by @Georgia_McBride and @YALitChat on Wednesdays, 9 P.M. EST
- **#LITCHAT:** An open networking session between readers with books and authors. Hosted by @litchat on Mondays, Wednesdays, and Fridays, 4–5 P.M. EST

When participating in or simply observing a chat, all your tweets should follow one of the hashtags used. Using the primary hashtag (#scifichat, #YALitChat, etc.) is enough to track with the discussion. If you are mentioning Twitter Chats on other platforms, you should use corresponding hashtags for tracking purposes.

Twitter Parties

Hosted by the author or a third party, with everyone using an agreed-upon hashtag, Twitter parties are similar to Twitter chats. The difference is that Twitter parties tend to double with the use of contests: participants (people who actively tweet or retweet content under the official hashtag) are entered into giveaways. Instead of happening on a weekly basis, these online events tend to happen before or after recent book releases, special events hosted by authors, and topics specific to the author who is hosting the Twitter party. If you are mentioning Twitter parties on other platforms, you should use corresponding hashtags for tracking purposes.

The most effective hashtags for parties are compact and easy to remember. Instead of a Twitter party hosted by #MinistryOfPeculiarOccurrences, it's hosted by #MoPO.

Proper Use of Hashtags

Accurate and consistent hashtagging of your content is good practice across a number of networks. The hashtag symbol has become a way to facilitate searching and indexing on social media platforms. People who are searching for a particular topic find them useful. When a hashtag is *trending*, it means it is being searched a lot and used often. Hashtags do come with some simple rules. Don't string too many words together, unless it is for comedy. For example, #mybookisawesomeandyoushouldbuyit is not going to get you anywhere, but it will make fans chuckle a bit.

Hashtags need to be accurate and to sensibly describe your content. Hijacking a popular or trending topic that doesn't accurately describe what you are doing (another form of "trolling") is a terrible idea. Such tactics inevitably backfire.

How so?

When popular brand name pizza DiGiorno used the hashtag #whyIstayed (which was about women and domestic violence) to advertise its pizza, the backlash was horrible. They had to respond with "A million apologies. Did not read what the hashtag was about before posting," which, in admitting DiGiorno was oblivious to the hashtag's intent, makes a bad situation worse.

Understanding what a hashtag is referencing before posting or contributing is always a good idea. If you have no idea, or just want to be sure you're not using someone else's hashtag, then visit tagdef. com. There you can find out what certain hashtags mean, or even define your own. Just check out one we created earlier.[1]

However, as useful as hashtags are, you can go overboard with them and lose the message you are trying to communicate. Stick to five hashtags in one post at the most. On Twitter, keep it to two.

Here are some good writerly tags for connecting with your readers: #FridayReads, #BookGiveaway, #MustRead, #StoryFriday, #LitChat, #FreeBook, #Kindle, and #Nook. And don't forget you can also hashtag your genre (#YA). If you are looking to network with other authors, try one of the following: #AmWriting, #AmEditing, #WriterWednesday, #AskAuthor, #IAN1, or #AuthorAlliance.

TAKING P!NK'S ADVICE: FACEBOOK PARTIES

> I'm comin' up so you better get this party started
> Get this party started on a Saturday night
> Everybody's waiting for me to arrive …

You know, that sassy rock star P!nk is absolutely right—people love a party, even an online one, so it's not surprising that advertisers have picked up on the chance to rally people online for a Facebook party. Direct marketers such as Avon and Jamberry were the first to catch onto the possibilities, but that doesn't mean that writers can't get in on the fun and create some visibility for their book titles in the process.

Before announcing your party, ask yourself first, what you are celebrating? No one celebrates an ordinary day of the week; they celebrate *milestone* events. As a writer, the biggest event of the season should be your book birthday, but you could also host an event for bundling your books together, a Kickstarter campaign for an anthology, or a

---

1 https://tagdef.com/mopo

cover reveal. Be careful you don't tire out your guests with too many parties in the course of one year.

As with a party that you would throw in your off-line life, the planning of an online party is important. Here are some questions you need to ask yourself before you announce your next bash to the world.

What Date?

You want to find one that doesn't clash with major holidays like Black Friday, Veteran's Day, or anything that could annoy or prevent your guests from attending. That doesn't mean that you can't plan your party around major days; for instance, the weeks before Christmas would be a great time to have a party to celebrate your holiday-themed book.

If you're doing a book release, you can decide to either build up excitement the week before the book comes out, or try and generate sales during the week after.

What Time?

Think about your readers, the location of your target audience, and if time zones come into play. The most recent *Ministry of Peculiar Occurrences* event was timed to be late in an evening and ran for four hours, until midnight EST. That way our readers on the West Coast could still join in, too. You are never going to be able to find an optimal time for everyone all over the world, but you can adjust it so that there is at least a chance for your international readers to find the party.

What Sort of Decorations?

Set up your event from your author page. Under More/Event/Create Event, input the date and time, and make it look pretty with a header image.

What Do I Serve?

You can't have food, but you can still have goodies to attract the guests. No one in the neighborhood is going to come unless you give them a reason, so consider things to give away. Be creative. Give away signed books or items related to your book. Steampunk writers give away tea. Fairytale urban fantasy writers give away apple-related items for Snow White, or hair products for Rapunzel. Romance writers give away jewelry. Think about your book, its theme, and your target audience. Keep it fun!

Whom Do You Invite?

Guests are important, but author guests can bring a crowd. If you are just starting off in the author space (think of it as being new to your neighborhood), then you might not have met many fellow writers. Obviously, if you've been to a few conferences, have made contacts online, or have a writers group, you are starting off with an advantage—if you want to include author guests. That doesn't mean you can't invite people if you're new; just be aware that a stranger asking is not the same as someone guests feel a connection with. However, politely asking people in a similar genre who are also starting off can't hurt. Bear in mind that you are also offering them a way to promote their own books.

Once author guests have said yes, find a good time for them to be on. You'll want ten- to fifteen-minute slots for guests to promote and interact, but also allow some buffer time so you can circulate and talk about your work.

The Big Night: Party Time!

As the date of the event approaches, there is still some work to do to make sure your event goes off with a bang.

Promotion

Spread the word, not just on Facebook, but on all your social media networks. Reach out to your author guests to help get the word out, and make sure you give them enough time to do so. Promotion should be around two weeks to a month out—any further out risks people forgetting, but if you promote too close to the event, then people can't plan to be there at your party. The more the merrier, after all.

Preparation

Before the event, make sure you have your timetable sorted out, as well as some prepared activities and information to keep the party flowing. For your author guests, make sure you have introductions ready to go. Be personable and welcoming. For the interludes where you plan to talk, have some prepared quotes from the books, questions, and, best of all, images. That way if things should start to flag or go quiet, you are only a cut-and-paste away from keeping people entertained.

Kick Off

When the night begins, you might want to make sure you are comfortable with virtual refreshments (or real ones) at hand, because a good Facebook party can fly by. Stay close to your computer or tablet, make sure you are there to answer questions, welcome people who arrive, and keep the conversation flowing.

Limber up your fingers, too, as you will be typing fast and hard. Hey, no one ever said being a host was easy!

Having chosen the prizes for the party, you can run contests in several ways: randomly picking people in the party room, perhaps a quiz based on your book (or something related, if it isn't out yet), or rewarding the guest who comes up with the best casting of your book's dream movie. Keep your questions and trivia simple, though. Nothing is more awkward than a competition where no one wins!

The End

Don't forget to say "thank you" to your guests and author guests. Before the party is over, remind people of the essential information: where to find your book, relevant dates and times concerning its release, and your website location, so if they have more questions, they know how to find you.

PLANNING MAKES PERFECT: BEFORE THAT SOCIAL MEDIA EVENT

Before attending Facebook or Twitter parties, or appearing as a "featured guest" at these events, have on hand precrafted posts. Concentrate on questions or topics that might get the conversation started again, and if tweets allow for space, have images ready to upload. Anticipate some of the questions readers might ask you:

- If your book were made into a movie, who would play _____?
- Where do you get your inspiration?
- Who are your favorite authors?
- Why do you write [your genre]?

Make certain you publicize when and where special online events will be taking place. Publicize your chats and parties across your blog, your podcast, and other platforms. People do not randomly appear for these events—they wait to hear from you.

Finally, especially if you are the special guest or are hosting a social media event, make certain you have all you need at arm's length. Have a drink close by. Make sure you've gone to the bathroom before go time. Once the event starts, don't leave your chair. The conversation will fly fast and furious.

ATTRIBUTION, NOT IMITATION, IS THE SINCEREST FORM OF FLATTERY

Being a good participant in social media means sometimes going the extra mile. If you do end up reposting pictures of cosplay (where people dress up as their favorite comic book, video game, or book characters), or someone else's travel adventures, retain any attribution the image came with. People who create things—and authors are part of that tribe—like to be credited for their work.

If there is an awesome image you really want to post, but it has been stripped of attribution, then you can go the extra mile. Put on your deerstalker hat and seek out the missing information.

It's actually easier than you think. Google is once again your friend. Go to Google's Search by Image feature.[2] Click on Try it Now, then click on the camera image in the right-hand corner, and either paste the URL of the image or upload an image. Click Search, and Google will do its best to help you find the original owner.

---

2 http://www.google.com/insidesearch/features/images/searchbyimage.html

It may seem like a bother, but it's the way you will cultivate a professional image.

The same goes for memes and motivationals—check the source. No one likes to have a reader say, "Einstein did not actually say that."

If this kind of research seems like too much, just stick to posting links and images you bought or made yourself.

SEEK OUT YOUR AUDIENCE

Every book has a target audience, but it won't come beating on your door. The truth is you have to find out where your people are, and go to them. Think about yourself and your book; where do you best fit?

If you still don't have an idea, look at where authors in your genre are concentrating. Do they appear to be having success on these platforms? Start building your community of readers in those places.

HAVE A PLAN

The leading cause of failure on social media is jumping on platforms without any idea of what to do. Social media is not something you do because "everyone else is doing it." You do it because you have something to accomplish.

When you set up a blog, ask yourself how often you intend to blog. Will you use Facebook to promote your blog? How often will you post on Facebook or Twitter? Will you go beyond these three sites and work with Tumblr? Google+? What will your voice be? Will you be all business, or will you pepper in personal thoughts? The more you map out your plan, the more focused your online platform will be.

These tips provide a great foundation for social media initiatives. Applying them to your networks can make your platform easier to develop and build, and make your signal strong and reliable. When you use social media to its full potential, you are actually building and developing your *brand*. Social media can help to define your brand.

The scary thing about brands, though, is that they are fragile and easily damaged. As important as it is to know what to do with social media, it is equally important to know what not to do. When you have the right strategy, most, if not all, of the missteps can easily be avoided.

FOCUS ON MAINTAINING A SIGNAL, NOT CREATING NOISE

When talking about social media and social networking, you may hear the term *signal-to-noise ratio*. Signal-to-noise refers to the quality of your statuses and updates. If you are constantly advertising or promoting something in your feed, your audience may tune out your updates, and so they are considered "noise." Updates that your audience genuinely cares about or interacts with are referred to as your "signal." When it comes to social media, it is easy to slip into noise mode. Signal is all about quality and what you deliver to your network.

So how do you avoid becoming *that* author?

Make a connection with your fan base through articles that capture the imagination. Share what you do when you are not writing. Do you have a passion for classical theater, B movies, or fashion? Tap into one of those topics. Post images, video, and your own blog articles on what it is that captures your attention or helps you unwind. Post this kind of content alongside interesting news articles rooted in your genre. On your fifth post, go ahead and do a quick promotion for your book. When a new review appears for it, share it on Facebook and Twitter. Celebrate with the community. You want to aim for a ratio of one promotional post to every five, or three promos out of every ten. People who follow you on networks will know that while you are there to promote your book, you are not there to do only that. You're a real person with real interests and passions outside of writing.

These are all practices that we have seen writers carry out across networks, many of them finding success in creating strong *street teams* (fans who love to talk to others about your books and who help you make the sale) for their works out in the world, and coming soon to both brick-and-mortar and online bookstores. Sadly, though, the success stories of social media are not what drove us to write this book. This particular social media guide is born out of our frustration, anger, and outright surprise when authors get online and make a mess of things. Our inspiration comes from the writers who don't know when to quit pitching their books, when to walk away from an argument, and when not to say a damn thing.

To the overly aggressive author on the Internet, this one's for you.

ANTISOCIAL MEDIA: WHAT TO AVOID IN ONLINE PROMOTION AND NETWORKING

There are a lot of things that you can get right in social media, but it is easy to get things wrong if you don't know what you are doing. Even if you do know what you are doing, you can still make mistakes. There's a difference between stumbling (which you can easily recover from) and hitting the ground hard, face first.

Forgetting the "Social" Aspect of Social Media

Many writers in social media tend to accept the bad advice of gurus who say that every tweet, Facebook, blog post, and post on Tumblr should be an advertisement for their next book. It is not uncommon to see this, and this is not how you build a platform or broaden a network. This is merely adding noise to your signal (as we defined above), so much noise that your followers will essentially tune you out. Keep your promotional posts under control. They should not become the sole voice and purpose of your social platforms.

Another rule of thumb in social media is to establish yourself as an individual and to invest time in building your network. The key is to do so in a smart and diplomatic manner. The best way to break this rule is to make your first communication on Twitter a direct message (DM) that encourages others to join your Facebook Page.

Social media is about you, but it should not be *all* about you.

Scraping: The Fastest Way to Get Yourself Kicked Out of the Pool

Yes, we are going to talk about scraping again. Why? Because it happens so frequently, and because it's so bad for your professional reputation.

The lure of the Dark Side is strong. Maybe you have one week when you simply feel like you have nothing interesting to say. But, hey, that wacky Chuck Wendig just wrote a brilliant post on most frequently asked writing questions. It's out there on the Internet, so it's fair game. You might be thinking, *I comment on Chuck's blog, so we're pals. He won't mind. I'll just cut and paste the post into my blog and ...*

No!

Seriously—scraping will give you a bad name and make you enemies in the writing world. However, scraping should not be confused with its kinder, more community-minded cousin, syndication. Scraping is taking the whole post and dropping it onto your page complete.

Here's a word that's synonymous with scraping: *plagiarism.* That is what scraping is, essentially.

You might even mention the original author's name or include his link, but that is not a pass in this instance. You have just stolen content, and eyeballs, from the creator of that content. The link back is worthless, since viewers just got all the good juice from your page. Remember that *syndication* is when a *portion* of the blog post (the first paragraph, or two, at the most) is pasted with proper attribution and the link back to the original blogger. That makes for happy content creators. Scraping will get you a bad reputation, and no invitations to the author's next birthday party.

And if you think authors and content creators don't notice these things, well, you're wrong there, too.

Friends at Wholesale: The Perils of Purchasing Likes or Followers

Many social media gurus encourage "investing" in your platforms, usually followed by the line "I can help you triple your Twitter followers for the low, low price of ..."

Inflated numbers on platforms look impressive, but it costs a lot for tens of thousands of Likes on Facebook and nameless, faceless Followers on Twitter. Purchased Likes originate from *Like farms,* companies that pay their employees to Like hundreds upon hundreds of pages of various products, personalities, and services featured on social networks. These Like farms fill your statistics with numbers but do not take any active role or have interaction with your community. While you suddenly appear to have those "rock star" statistics, these inflated numbers burn through your advertising budget on Facebook and cost you more when it comes time to boost posts. Concerning Twitter, these bulk Followers are nothing more than automated "bots" that tweet nonsense, junking up your incoming tweets and making it harder and harder for you to track your main Twitter feed. Other popular Twitter accounts purchased in bulk include pornography sources and malware carriers. Follower purchases on Instagram will spam your feed with a sudden dumping of images, many of them random, innocuous posts of what that company is selling, turning your Instagram feed into a Sears catalog.

Not only do these accounts distance you from your network, limiting your interaction to only those who directly mention you, but they can damage your online brand, as these bots will find unsuspecting targets from your own networks. Be wary with these paid services, as they lead to nothing but noise.

Focusing on the *Quality*, not the *Quantity*: The Statistics Game

You will be told time and time again (most of the time from the people selling the above-mentioned Likes and Followers) how important it is to have the numbers on your platforms. There are plenty of authors who love touting their five- and six-figure numbers. Simply ask these social media hoarders exactly what they do with these numbers. Or, if you want to be more to the point, ask them, "Exactly how do you communicate with 100,000 people?"

You don't. You talk *at* them.

It is always a good idea to check people who are requesting to follow you on networks. When a user starts to follow you on Instagram, for instance, check the account to see if it is an actual person with a story or a product to sell. Look at the accounts, evaluate the feed, and see if this is someone you want to connect with.

You should also check Facebook accounts when people send a Friend Request to your personal account or Group. When the request arrives, click on the account. Here's what you want to look for in a phony account:

- Activity on the Timeline: When did this account go live? What is being shared on the feed? Is she sharing pictures?
- How many Groups does this person like? If he is a member of more than fifty groups, consider it a red flag.
- What is she Liking on Facebook? Many of the spammers will Like the same game and/or products they promote.

BOOKMARK

On Instagram, a telltale sign of a bogus or malicious account is the follow that happens in response to images that are weeks or even years old on your feed. Following the Like back to where it originated will either reveal an old friend or recent follower you've met and want to reconnect with, or a spammer with something to sell. Be cautious when older images in your feed are suddenly getting some love.

The social media gurus will encourage you to follow and follow blindly, but it is always good to check out the source first. What will this person bring to your network? Is this someone who will participate or simply promote, using your network?

Message Garbled, Say Again: Avoid Nonsense in Your Feed

Inspirational quotes. Retweets. Promotions of your latest book.

If these are occasionally in your feed, that's one thing. If any of these *are* your feed, you are missing the point of Twitter. Or Instagram. Or Tumblr.

People follow you on social networks to find out more about you, not about who you follow or what other people have said. Whether you are filling your Instagram with an endless parade of products or having your Facebook and Google+ echo your Twitter account, make your content original and understandable.

A Garden Gone to Seed: Leaving Accounts Unattended

From his time in the information security field, Tee can tell you that many InfoSec professionals are opposed to a lot of the networks covered in this book, as security tends to be overlooked when these services are developed and brought online. The vulnerabilities present on Facebook, Tumblr, and other social media platforms are a genuine concern, as social networks are easily commandeered by hackers, especially when accounts are left unattended and underutilized. Keep your account active with daily postings, and watch for any odd activity or suspicious postings appearing under your name. If you find that a platform is not for you, it is best to delete the account completely rather than to leave it live. Lack of activity on any social media platform opens your brand to damage.

Suspicious Minds: Responding to Peculiar Messages

There is another method hackers use to gain control of social media contacts. It is a method of infiltration called "social engineering." You see this most often in e-mails supposedly from PayPal and banks informing you that your account will be shut down in twenty-four hours if you do not visit a link provided in the e-mail. On Facebook and Twitter, social engineering most commonly happens in direct messaging. Usually the messages will say something along the lines of "LOL Have u seen this vid?" followed by a link. On rare occasions, these messages appear from accounts you recognize (possibly someone who has been hacked), but they mostly come from strangers (bots). Anytime you receive messages that appear to be sent by people who don't have time to spell out words, chances are the account has been compromised. Contact that user (on a public channel) and inform the person (politely) that you received a strange direct message.

Come On Feel the Noise: Oversharing

Have you come across images that read "You are [insert iconic character]" in your Facebook feeds lately? These are images produced by Livingly Media (formerly known as Zimbio, Inc.), a digital media company that manages lifestyle sites for desktop and mobile audiences. The quizzes, sponsored by Livingly, ask a variety of questions about your location, your lifestyle, and your interests, and from this information, the quiz names you as Captain Kirk, Harry Potter, Katniss Everdeen, Princess Leia, or some other favorite character of literature or film.

Did you ever stop to ask what permissions were granted for these images? Whether the actors and actresses used in these images have been compensated? And how do these questions result in your being named an iconic character?

They don't. This is called *data mining*.

It's not quite the same as social engineering, but it is a bait-and-switch approach to getting people to take market surveys and for building mailing lists that are sold to other parties. Social media is about sharing, and it's more than okay to share, but there is a point where you can share too much online, opening yourself to a variety of annoyances ranging from spam to identity theft.

When it comes to sharing, you must decide where you draw the line in what you will share and what you won't. Social media is your platform for your works and for you as an author. It is not your therapist's couch. *Oversharing,* that sudden outpour of emotion and in-your-face position-taking, can not only alienate your online network of contacts, both personal and professional, but can also reflect poorly on you.

Oversharing is nothing new in social networking, but it is far too easy a trap to fall into. Do you want to become known as "that guy" or "that girl"? To help prevent taking a misstep, the first and foremost question to ask yourself every single time you are ready to post is:

"Should I be sharing this?" It would be great to say that people think before they post, but sadly, some are more about sending out a snappy, witty update or sharing with the world than considering who's watching their feeds.[3]

Social networking has become a way that we communicate with people, both one-on-one and around the world, but there are limits. To sharing. To connecting. To communicating. These limits are set by you. Social media platforms serve as fantastic outlets, so long as you approach them responsibly and reasonably. Remember that your brand and your reputation are at stake, therefore your social media activity warrants your *full* attention. Social networking is an *investment* in your career and should be cared for and cultivated. Go beyond networking and build a community around your work. This community can become your street team for future book releases and events you will be attending, increasing your profile both in the online world and the real one.

Good luck, and good hunting!

---

3 http://www.businessinsider.com/twitter-fired-2011-5?op=1

SOCIAL MEDIA FOR WRITERS

WordPress

SETTING UP A WORDPRESS ACCOUNT

BOOKMARK

Security starts with you. Always create passwords that are alphanumeric: made up of a mix of numbers, uppercase and lowercase letters, and symbols. The longer the password, the more difficult it is to hack. So if the site lets you have fifteen characters, you should make your password fifteen characters. Keep these passwords in an encrypted file on a flash drive, and keep the drive in a safe place.

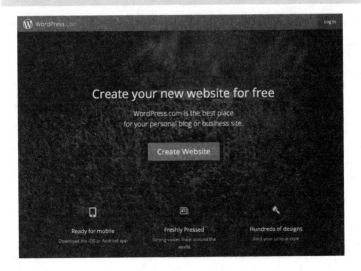

1. Go to WordPress.com and click on the Create Website button.
2. Give your site a name.

3. Enter your e-mail address, your username, and a password. When coming up with a password, you want to pick something easy to remember but tricky to figure out so no one can hack into your account. A mix of letters, numbers, and characters is always good. For example, instead of *Richmond Writer* for your password, you could use *r!chm0nDwr1t3r*, making it memorable but difficult to crack.

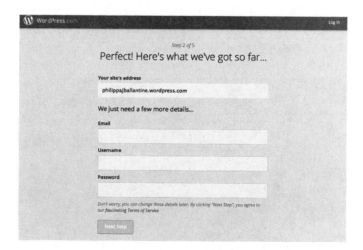

4. Now WordPress will ask you if you want a custom address. You can always set up a simple, easy-to-remember URL through 1and1.com, GoDaddy.com, or a similar registrar service, and then have that URL reroute your visitors to this location. You can also have WordPress.com take care of this URL for $18 per year. Decide if you want your username to be your name, a keyword, or an acronym.

5. Next you can choose one of WordPress's themes.

6. You can then either select Create Blog or give WordPress Business or WordPress Premium a test run. For this exercise, click on Create Blog, but know that you can upgrade at any time. Compare plans and consider your options if your blog begins to gain traction.

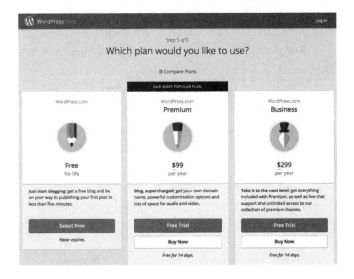

7. Once the blog is created, click on the Dashboard link. The Dashboard is a one-stop interface that can give you a rundown of what is happening on your blog, as well as tell you what is happening

with other WordPress.com users. Statistics, Activity, and even a Quick Draft interface are offered for your blogging needs.

8. Go to the top-right of your Dashboard GUI. You will see a blank profile icon. Click on the blank profile option, which looks like a picture of a person. The WordPress Profile is necessary for when you want to post across the WordPress network and the Internet. The more you can tell people about yourself, the easier it will be for people to connect with you.

9. Review your Account Options. Under Settings, you can edit your Account Options, your Password, and the like. Here you can review the various options and little touches that make a complete profile.

10. In the Web address field, enter your website address and click on the Gravatar Profile link offered. A *gravatar* is a globally recognized avatar, an image people use to represent themselves online. It is a little picture that appears next to a person's name when interacting with websites. You create this profile only once, and your gravatar image will automatically appear when you participate in any gravatar-enabled site.

11. Click on the Sign In icon to authorize Gravatar.

12. Complete your Gravatar and WordPress profile. The best images are usually square, no larger than 600 × 600 pixels, RGB, and either saved as a PNG or a JPEG file. The images can be cropped online using the Gravatar interface. Upload your image and click on My Profile to return to your Settings and select Public Profile to fill in the details.

Up and Running

Congratulations! You have an account with WordPress. Your blog is still up and running, but you have no blog posts and no content online. You're going to want to make a post introducing yourself and your future blog. This inaugural post can be as detailed and as informative as you like, but the more people who know about you and what your blog is about, the more likely you will pick up subscribers. This blog will serve as your foundation for your social media platform.

GETTING TO KNOW WORDPRESS

Writing Your First Blog Post

1. From your Dashboard, go to Posts > Add New or simply select the New Post option from the top-right of your browser. You will notice that your Dashboard offers a few shortcuts to creating and editing posts. Use the methods that work best for you.

2. Single-click in the Title field and type Welcome to My Writer's Blog.

3. Select the text in the Post field and replace it with the following:

   > This is my first blog entry. I am now officially getting my hands dirty in social media, learning how initiatives like blogging work, but I will be getting into Facebook, Twitter, and other networks as well. It's going to be a long day, but I can see now just how easy it is to write for a blog. How cool is that?

4. On the left-hand side you will see an option called Categories. Click on Add New Category and create a Writing category. Go on and create three more categories: What I'm Reading, Out in the World, and Fun Facts for the Day.

5. Single-click on the drop-down menu for Parent Category and select the Writing category. Now create Fiction and Nonfiction categories. *Subcategories* can be listed with parent categories in your blog posts. Categories and subcategories help search filters work more efficiently. So if you tell the WordPress search engine on your blog to show only the Writing or Fiction posts, other posts are temporarily hidden.

6. Select Writing and Fun Facts of the Day as categories for the post you just created.

7. Scroll down to Tags, and in the provided field, type in the following keywords:

blog, introduction, social media, nonfiction, what I'm doing, Facebook, Twitter

8. Click the Add button. *Tags* not only help out search filters, but they also work with search engines to find your posts easily. Use between ten to twenty tags to increase your likelihood of being found (and found easily) by those searching for specific topics.

9. Single-click the Publish button.

And you are blogging. Just like that. Now, a few housekeeping duties await.

Working with Pages

You have successfully created your first post. Before you move forward, we need to take care of some odds and ends that bloggers new to WordPress tend to overlook. These little touches are simple to employ and should be taken care of right away, just to avoid clutter and confusion.

1. Return to your Dashboard. If you are logged into WordPress, you will be able to access your Dashboard while viewing your blog.

2. In the Settings section, select the General option. In Settings, you edit your blog title, set time zones (important for scheduling), and address other details that may seem nit-picky but are important to keeping your blog efficient and reliable.

3. Edit your Tagline to read:
   The Official Blog of Author [Your Name Here]

4. Set your time zone and post formats.

5. Click the Save Changes button.

6. Select the Pages option. Click on the About title or select the Edit option, and replace the text found in the Post field with the following:
   This blog is the official website of author [Insert Your Name Here]. Here you'll find my musings and occasional rants about a writer's life. You can also find me on various social networks, such as xxx.

7. In the title field, change the current title to:
   Who Am I?

8. Click on the Update button, then select the All Pages option from the Pages menu.
9. Click the Quick Edit option for the Who Am I? page and disable the Comments option by single-clicking the checkboxes.
10. Single-click the Update button.

Post vs. Page

The difference between a *Post* and a *Page* is that a Post is more dynamic and lets you update your blog. Depending on your Preferences, your Posts appear on the main page of your website, are categorized, and get syndicated across other RSS feeds. A Page, while still dynamic in how it is updated, is more static. It should display such information as who you are, what you or your organization is known for, how to contact you, and the like. A Page is a permanent part of your blog where information rarely changes, but it can be edited and updated, just like a regular blog post, and while you want interaction with your Posts, it is best not to have Comments active for Pages.

CREATING CONTENT

Now that your blog is currently void of some outstanding "Beginner's Blog" traits, you can focus on letting people know a little bit about who you are in the blogosphere.

Making a Good First Impression

Now that you have successfully made your first post, edited your About Page, and removed some of the other default settings to make this blog manageable, let's dive deeper into the amazing features of blogging.

Scheduling Blog Posts

WordPress offers users the ability to post news and events even when they are unable to get to their computers. Blog posts, composed ahead of time, can be scheduled for automatic posting. This is a terrific feature to take advantage of when weighing busy schedules against the weekly demands of a blog.

1. Single-click the My Dashboard tab. If you are logged into WordPress, you will still be able to access your Dashboard while viewing your blog.
2. In the left-hand toolbar, roll over the Posts option and select the Add New option.
3. For the title of this blog post, type in the following: *Scheduling Blog Posts.*
4. In the Post field, type in the following (or something like it*): I'm not able to get to WordPress right now. Tea time, you know. So I am actually scheduling this post for a later time. This means that while I am away from the computer, my blog will automatically update. Pretty freakin' cool, huh?*
5. To the right-hand side of the blog interface, you see the Publish Immediately option. Single-click on Edit to access the scheduling interface.
6. Set the various drop-down menus to today's date, but set the time stamp thirty minutes from the current time.
7. Click OK to exit the timing options and then click on Schedule.

You can check back fifteen minutes later, but you will see if you click on the All Posts option that your blog post is now scheduled and waiting to go. Keep this option in mind if you are working with reoccurring features on your blog or welcoming guest bloggers to create content. You can "collect" posts ahead of time and schedule a week's worth of content while organizing articles for the following week.

Incorporating Images and Links

With all the details in place on the back end, let's add some details to what visitors to your blog will see. Dropping images into your blog is easy and adds a nice touch to your posts. You can use a variety of formats for images, but the preferred formats are:

- JPEG (Joint Photographic Experts Group)
- PNG (Portable Network Graphics)

You can incorporate images from your computer or link to images located on other websites. And speaking of other websites, let's create a link from your blog to another website.

1. Single-click the My Dashboard tab at the top-left of your browser. If you are logged into WordPress, you will still be able to access your Dashboard while viewing your blog.
2. In the left-hand toolbar, roll over the Posts option of your browser and single-click on the All Posts option.
3. Single-click the Scheduling Blog Posts post.
4. Place your cursor at the beginning of the post and single-click the Add Media button.
5. Single-click the Insert from URL option and enter in the following options:

    a. **IMAGE URL:** http://teemorris.com/images/wordpress.jpg
    b. **ALT TEXT:** Tea Time with WordPress
    c. **ALIGNMENT:** Left

6. Single-click the Insert into Post option.

BOOKMARK

When you link your blog post to an image located on a server other than your own, a preview of the image will appear in this WordPress window. This is an indication that the image link is good.

7. Once the image appears in the blog post, single-click the image and then click the Edit Image icon at the top-left corner of the image.
8. In this interface, click on the Advanced Settings tab. Enter 10 (pixels) in both the Horizontal and Vertical Space, and then click the Update option.
9. Highlight WordPress in your blog entry.

10. Single-click the chain link icon. In the URL field, enter: http://wordpress.com.
11. Click Update to accept the URL for the link.
12. Click Update to make changes to your blog post live.

You can now add visual media to your words. Visuals assist in getting your message across. Keep in mind that media of any kind should help, not hinder, the message of your blog. Adding an array of unrelated images might steer your audiences off target, so be certain that any accompanying photos and media relate directly to the intent of your post.

Tumblr

SETTING UP A TUMBLR ACCOUNT

Tumblr is one of the easiest social media platforms to work with. To set up an account, follow these instructions:

1. Go to www.tumblr.com, enter a valid e-mail address, and make a username—keep it simple, using your author name is a good idea—and create a password.
2. Once you tell Tumblr how old you are, accept the terms of service, and prove you are not a robot, it will create an account for you.
3. Tumblr will then ask you what you are interested in and prompt you to start following five blogs. You can follow some of the suggested blogs or search for others using terms such as "writing" and "authors," or type in your genre. The more you follow, the

more you'll feel a part of the community, so feel free to select more than five.

4. You will have to confirm your e-mail address in order to customize your account.

5. Click on the head icon in the top-left corner and then click on "Edit Appearance."

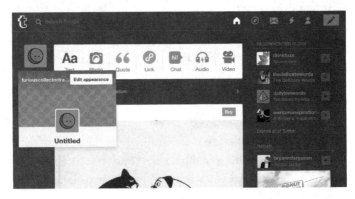

6. Let's make your Tumblr look more like you want it to. Use an avatar, and then tweak the color scheme. Title and description are optional but useful.

7. Next you can download the Tumblr app for IOS, Android, or a Windows Phone. You don't have to do it now, but it is a great app to have at your fingertips.

And *voila*, there you are in your Dashboard. Don't panic: This is not how the viewing public will see your Tumblr, but it is where you will be spending some time managing and sprucing up your account and blog.

Though this initial setup generates your primary blog, you can in fact have multiple blogs in the form of secondary accounts, and/or add pages to any of these blogs. You might want to consider using your primary blog as your writer account, with different pages for your series. Or you might want to

have secondary blogs for your series, especially if you are co-writing them. Again, you may be splitting your brand too much, so decide how fractured you want your Tumblr content to be.

GETTING TO KNOW TUMBLR

Let's go ahead and get familiar with the Tumblr controls. There are several key areas.

The Top Bar

- **HOME:** This will take you back to the main dashboard and your stream.
- **EXPLORE:** This will bring you to the browse section of Tumblr. Here you can see trending topics, categories, and staff picks. It is a great place to find blogs to follow.
- **MAIL:** This is where you will get messages, questions, submissions, and fan mail from your Tumblr followers. Keep an eye on this icon to alert you to these valuable interactions.
- **LIGHTNING BOLT:** This will take you to your activity page, where you can see how engaged people are with what you are posting, your biggest fans (people who engage or repost your posts the most), and the latest comments on your posts. It's fun to watch the graphs here.
- **HEAD ICON:** This is the home base for all of your content. This shows you how many posts you have made, how many follow-

ers you have, what activity has occurred since you last checked (along with a neat chart of how your posts are doing), and how many items you have lined up in your queue. Most important, it offers the ability to customize your page. Clicking on the head icon will allow you to change the appearance of your page. Much like WordPress, Tumblr has themes—these are frameworks for the page, so you can easily set up the look of your blog. Some are free, and some are available to purchase, but there are so many themes that finding something for yourself and your genre is a definitely possibility. In the Customize menu, you will see what your Tumblr looks like to the public. On the left, you will see your options. These will vary according to the theme you have selected. You can use this to add static pages to your Tumblr. You might, for example, want to have a separate page for an About page or perhaps a list of events you are attending.

- **THE PEN:** Click this for all the options you need to post content. The next bar is our favorite.

The Content Bar

This is where you get to do the fun stuff (post your own content to Tumblr!). The tools here are fairly self-explanatory: Text, Photo, Quote (great for dropping samples of your work into your feed), Link, Chat (so you can ask your followers questions, a great way to encourage engagement), Audio, and Video.

Each of these offers different advanced options, but the most useful ones are Schedule and Add to Queue. These are some of Tumblr's best features for you as an author, since they allow you to target a post to go live at an important moment—say on a book launch date—or pop a post in a feed to be delivered on a regular schedule. Remember your readers like consistency with their content!

Now that you have your Tumblr up and running the way you want it, let's fill it with some content.

POSTING TO TUMBLR

Adding your own content to your Tumblr stream is always the preferable option, so let's take a quick look at the ways you can do it:

- **TEXT:** Give it a title, and write your content in the field at the bottom. You can also format your text in a variety of ways, including making those all-important links back to your site or where to buy your book.
- **PHOTO:** Here you can upload up to ten photos, or take one directly with the camera in your computer. Remember: Images are your best friend on Tumblr.
- **QUOTE:** Use this to add little teasers from your work-in-progress or novel that's about to release. Make sure they are punchy quotes that express the content of your book or main character.
- **URL:** This is where you link to your WordPress site or to reviews of your books. Unfortunately, you can't use an image with this option, so you might want to use it sparingly.
- **CHAT:** Use this to solicit commentary and that important engagement. It can also be used to chat with your readers and ask them their opinions or about favorite characters, etc.
- **AUDIO:** This is where you would post podcasts, or recordings of your story. Samples of your audiobook would be an excellent choice to upload—just remember to keep them up to 10 MB and in MP3 format. You can search for a track to post, upload directly, or share from a URL. Do be sure to fill in all the fields and to have a good cover image for maximum impact.
- **VIDEO:** If you have a book trailer, this is where you can upload it directly (if it's 100 MB or less), or you can put in the code (say

SOCIAL MEDIA FOR WRITERS

from YouTube) or the URL where the video can be found. The same rules for filling all the fields apply.

No matter what you upload, do not forget to supply the relevant hashtags to draw attention to your post.

REBLOGGING

Sometimes you just don't have enough original content to feed the hunger of Tumblr, or you want to spread out what you do have. In our Ministry of Peculiar Occurrences Tumblr, we do three reblogs to one original post. Using this ratio, you will avoid constantly shouting "buy my book" into the void.

Reblogging also offers the advantage of building a following. Everyone whose post you reblog sees that you've reblogged their post, after all.

So let's have a go at reblogging some content.

The blogs you are following are now showing up in your dashboard in a stream, with the newest at the top. Find something useful and relevant to your audience.

At the bottom of the post are a few icons. The three dots on the left allow you to share the post on other social media networks, flag it, e-mail it, embed it, or get the permalink (a permanent link to the post). On the far right is the Heart icon, which is how you Favorite the post. It's a nice way to show a sense of community and will help your account get noticed, but reposting is even better.

The icon that we are really interested in is the middle one, which has two circling arrows. This is the icon that will post the item into your Tumblr feed. Clicking on it will bring the post you want to reblog up in full. Here you can add your own tags, put the post into your queue, schedule it, or post it right away. We would urge you to add your own commentary to the item before you post, just to let people know that you are not some robot mindlessly reposting items. For our steampunk series we usually try to say something that will link the item back to the series. If we see a vehicle the Ministry might use, we point that out. The point is to bring it back to your brand without hijacking the content. Always remember to leave whatever attribution there is on the post intact.

Podcasting

AN INTRODUCTION TO PODCASTING

Unlike most other social media outlets, podcasting requires specific hardware and software, which can be a daunting prospect for people, especially those who have never shopped for audio equipment. Where does one begin?

Nothing to worry about: We'll walk you through it.

First of all, an audio studio can come in a variety of shapes, sizes, and price tags. Your own setup can be kept economical and remain within a modest budget, or you can invest in something worthy of Audible.com. Whatever setup you envision for your podcasting endeavors, there are plenty of affordable options out there.

Let's begin with what kind of microphone is capturing your words. Microphones come in various shapes, sizes, and makes, all with varying benefits. Then you should determine the following:

- **HOW MUCH CAN YOU AFFORD TO SPEND?** Like everything in life, you get out what you put in, so the more money you spend, the better sound quality you can get out of your microphone. Consider the quality you need, before you put down your dollars on a microphone.
- **ARE YOU PLANNING TO USE THE MICROPHONE IN YOUR STUDIO OR OUT ON LOCATION?** A fancy, high-end shock-mounted model isn't going to cut it if you are doing an on-the-street or off-the-cuff podcast. Trying to make do with a lapel mic will not give you

the quality of sound expected in an Audible-quality recording. Consider your strategy and where you want to take your podcast—indoors or out.

- **WHAT EXACTLY DO YOU WANT THIS MIC TO DO?** Are you recording fiction, conducting interviews, or just kicking back with a fireside chat? Your choice of microphone rests on what you want to accomplish, so consider how you want to use your microphone.

With the answers to these three questions, your options at Amazon, BSW, and Guitar Center narrow a bit, but you still face many variations of microphones to choose from.

What are you looking for?

Affordable Microphones

Most affordable mics are Universal Serial Bus (USB) powered, and designed to plug into your computer and start recording moments after unboxing them. USB mics are available where electronics are sold.

Some USB microphones that are popular with podcasters include:

- **BLUE SNOWBALL:** This microphone can be found just about everywhere, ranging in price between $50 to $100. The quality of audio from the various models of Snowball is good. These are great starter microphones for authors entering the podcasting realm.
- **BLUE YETI:** From the makers of Snowball, the Yeti is a step up, usually listed in the $150 range. The Yeti offers a built-in headphone amplifier and controls on the device for headphone volume, pattern selection, mute, and microphone gain. A THX Certified Microphone, the Yeti captures a wider range of audio and vocal subtleties.
- **MARSHALL MXL 990 USB:** We use the MXL 990 condenser microphone for both desktop and remote recordings, so we can vouch for its abilities. The USB cousin works without mixers, preamps, or special studio gear. Simply plug the microphone into your com-

puter, and you can create pro-quality recordings. With a gold-sputtered diaphragm and a high-quality FET preamp, the MXL 990 USB comes in around $150. Guitar Center's MXL 990 USB kit, which includes a tripod, headphones, mic stand, and proper cables, sells for about $250. It's everything you need in just one purchase.

BOOKMARK

"Portable podcasting" faced many limits once upon a time, as small, built-in condenser mics struggled to offer quality of any kind. Now podcasters can take all their recording solutions on the go without fail with the Zoom H2n and H4n. These are lightweight, unobtrusive, all-in-one solutions for portable-podcast recording. Ranging in price from $150 to $200, both the H2n and H4n record audio directly to SD cards or can plug directly into your computer. With their built-in microphone through USB, they can record directly to MP3 format (in a variety of bit rate compressions) and to WAV format (also in a variety of bit rate settings). H4n goes even further, allowing for multitrack recording.

The H2n and H4n are fantastic solutions for professional audio producers, as well as for beginning podcasters who need a complete startup package.

Investing in High-End Microphones

For a cleaner sound for your podcast and the potential of breaking into professional-quality audiobook production, $50 to $100 mics will not deliver what you need. What truly makes a microphone is how you sound in it and how it reproduces the sound coming in. Based on the technology of the microphone itself, and how well it reproduces your voice, prices vary, but as you can see from our recommendations, plenty of high-quality microphones, able to pick up nuances in the human voice, fall into the range of affordability.

- **SHURE SM58:** When it comes to signature microphones—ones
  like you see everywhere—if you want that professional sound
  without the professional price tag, look no further than the Shure
  SM58. For nearly fifty years, this mic has been an industry favorite
  because of its durability and reliability. The SM58 works like a
  charm, recording on the street or in a studio. Podcasters love it
  for its affordability (it's available for $100).

- **SHURE SM7B:** Another industry standard that's found in many
  radio stations across the United States and around the world is
  the Shure SM7B. For $350, it is nothing less than an investment.
  This particular mic is optimized for in-studio recording, which
  is why it is used in so many radio stations and recording studios,
  but the SM7B, like the SM58 and most USB mics (not the MXL
  990USB), is a *dynamic* microphone. These types of microphones
  do not need any power from whatever mixer or preamps they are
  using in order to connect with the computer or recording device.
  They also record audio differently than other mics (which we are
  about to cover), and therefore capture different vocal nuances. Of
  the various microphones covered so far, the SM7B is the best of
  the bunch, offering you Audible-quality audio.

So far we have looked at dynamic microphones—durable, reliable
microphones of varying cost and quality. Recording in the studio,
though, is all about the details, and when you want that detail, it's
time to shop for a *studio condenser* microphone. Condenser mics work

very differently than dynamic ones. First, they are *phantom powered,* which means they receive an extra little electrical kick that helps them take in audio at their full potential. Phantom power comes from the mic's connection to the mixer, which supplies a constant boost to the condenser's sensitive diaphragm in order to catch details that dynamic mics miss. Condenser mics are also different because their delicate internal design makes them best for a stationary setup. If jostled around, plates inside the mic's housing can be knocked out of whack or damaged, causing problems in the pickup of the audio. The advantage to condenser microphones is that they pick up a wider spectrum of audio.

- **MARSHALL MXL 990:** As mentioned earlier, the 990 USB was the exception of those other USB models due to its being a studio condenser model. Not only is it available as a USB, but it also comes as a standard studio condenser microphone, a favorite of ours. Featuring the same gold-sputtered diaphragm as its USB counterpart, the standard MXL 990 comes in at around $100, complete with shock mount and carrying case. It's an inexpensive microphone with a bright sound, and it's worth every penny.
- **AKG PERCEPTION 120 AND 220:** We are big fans of the AKG Perception line and use it to this day in our *Shared Desk* podcast. The Perception 120 is a fantastic investment for just under $100, while the 220 comes in at $150. Both mics offer superior pickups and brilliant, rich audio quality. What make the Perceptions terrific investments are their built-in switchable attenuation pads and low-cut filter, which dampen any background noise in your home studio.

THE MIXING BOARD:
BRIDGING THE GAP BETWEEN MICROPHONE AND COMPUTER

If you're looking to have guests in the studio, or want to work with multiple inputs of audio or take advantage of phantom-powered studio condenser microphones, you will want to invest in a *mixing board.* What a mixing board (or mixer) does for your podcast is open up recording options such as using multiple microphones, recording acoustic instruments, and balancing sound to emphasize one voice over another or to balance both seamlessly.

The easiest way to look at a mixing board is as if you're partitioning your computer into different recording studios. But instead of calling them *studios,* these partitions are called *tracks*, and you can use any of those tracks for input *or* output of audio.

The easiest USB mixers to set up and get running on your computer cost $70 and go up from there. The cost increases with each additional track. The real advantage of a mixer is the ability to adjust various audio levels of multiple inputs independently in order to make the final signal sound even. Mixers also offer you the option of working with multiple mics, so if you have more than one speaker, you won't have to huddle around the same microphone or slide it back and forth as you take turns speaking.

Mixers can look a little intimidating with all those wacky knobs running up and down the interface. Some of the knobs deal with various frequencies in a voice and can deepen, sharpen, or soften the qualities of a voice. The knobs that are your primary concern are the ones that control your volume or *levels,* as the board labels them. The higher the level, the more input signal a voice gains when recording.

Hooking Up a Mixer to Your Computer

Once you have a section of your desk cleared off and reserved for your mixer, open the box containing your new mixer and make sure everything that should be there is there:

- USB mixer
- Power supply
- USB cable
- Instructions

Before hooking up anything, check the manufacturer's website for downloads (new drivers, upgrades to firmware, patches, and so on) needed for your digital board to work at its optimum level. USB mixers are so simple to set up that we can give these steps for both Mac and Windows machines:

1. Shut down your computer.
2. Connect the power supply to the back of the mixer and to an available wall socket or power strip.
3. Find an available USB port and plug your mixer into the computer. If your computer's ports are maxed out, we recommend setting up a USB hub for your other devices in order to free up one port. We do not recommend running your mixer through a hub, as doing so might affect the quality of the audio.
4. Plug the USB cable into the back of your mixer.
5. Connect your input devices (microphones, headphones, and the like) to the mixer.
6. Power up your mixer by turning on the Main Power and the Phantom Power switches.
7. Start your computer.

And that's it! You're ready to record with your USB or FireWire mixer. Now, with headphones on your head and some toying around, you will be able to set levels on your mixer that are good for recording.

BOOKMARK

The earlier mentioned H4n and the recent Zoom creation H6n, when hooked up to your computer, also double as *preamps*. The preamp works as a basic connection between your mics and your computer, and it provides phantom power to your condenser microphones. If you don't feel the need for a mixer or you just want to keep it simple, you may want to consider the all-in-one approach with the Zoom H4n or H6n.

WHAT'S NEXT: OTHER DETAILS FOR AN AUDIO STUDIO

A microphone and mixing board are the necessities in building a home audio suite, but there are a few more items you'll want to complete your recording studio. These add-ons are not essential to audio recording but can help you in producing a rock-solid audio production:

- **HEADPHONES:** Headphones help you monitor yourself as you record. By hearing your voice, you can catch any odd slip ups, slurred words, or mispronunciations before playback. The best kind of headphones are *closed-ear* headphones, and the *Sennheiser HD202* closed-ear headphones for around $20 offer everything you need for clean, clear audio monitoring.

BOOKMARK

We have been asked often about Bose Noise Cancelling stereo headphones for recording purposes. Bose makes an excellent pair of headphones, offering the highest quality for audio listening. Note, we say *listening*. Not *recording* and *editing*. Any headphones you see listed as "noise-cancelling" are going to be terrific for listening, but these kind of headphones aren't the best to use for recording and editing. You want to be able to hear the noise that these headphones cancel out so that you can eliminate it before a word is recorded. The best noise reduction and elimination happens before and during recording, not afterward. For podcast production, stick with closed-ear headphones sans noise-cancelling features.

- **CABLES:** As mentioned earlier, high-end microphones may arrive without cables. Check with a sales representative or the mic's documentation to find out what cables you need before you buy. Many of the microphones suggested here use a *3-pin XLR-to-XLR male-to-female* cable. The female end connects to the mic, and the male end, to the mixer. These cables begin at $9 and go up from there, depending on the length of the cord and quality of the input.

- **MICROPHONE STANDS:** If you invest in the Marshall MXL 990 (USB or XLR), you will receive a shock mount and an attachment for a mic stand, but no microphone stand. Believe us when we say that a good mic stand is worth the investment. A basic *desktop mic stand* can run you around $10, while a *boom mic stand* starts at around $100. The type of mic stand you invest in depends on how you want to work around it. With the simple stand, you're all set and ready to go without the extra hassle of positioning and securing a boom stand to your desk. The boom stand, though, frees up space on your desk, allowing for show notes and extra space for you to record and mix. Consult your budget to see which models are within your range.

You have the basics in place and the strategy to move forward. Now it is time to record, edit, and podcast.

APPENDIX D

Facebook

SETTING UP A FACEBOOK ACCOUNT

If you're not on Facebook, it's time to get on it. There are over 864 million active users. As an author, you need to use the platform to promote your work. So let's get you set up.

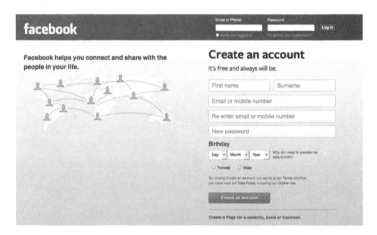

1. Go to Facebook.com and fill in all the fields to set up an account. Make sure you use your proper *author name* so people can find you. Be aware that Facebook's official rules say you should use your "authentic name." This has proved to be problematic with authors who use pen names or multiple names for different genres. Some authors choose to operate two profiles: one for their personal con-

tacts and one for their professional contacts. Others have a personal account from which they operate a Page as a professional author.

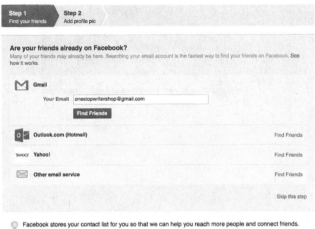

2. After you've filled in these fields, Facebook will try to find your friends. It will use Gmail, Outlook, Yahoo!, and other e-mail services to do so. You can skip this step if you are not comfortable doing this. You can always search for more friends later on.

3. Upload a profile picture.

4. Confirm your account. You are a new member of the Facebook family!

GETTING TO KNOW FACEBOOK

Facebook has many parts. It is, after all, one of the biggest and oldest social media platforms available. As you join and make Groups and Pages, it will get deeper. For now, let's look around this new platform.

On the top blue navigation bar, you will find all the information you inputted about yourself.

- **FACEBOOK ICON:** This will bring you back to your main page.
- **SEARCH BAR AND ICON:** Here you can look up people and Pages you might be interested in.
- **AVATAR:** Clicking on this will take you to your profile. Here you can make changes and add your Likes.

- **HOME:** Much like the Facebook icon, this button will take you back to your main feed and Page.
- **FIND FRIENDS:** Facebook wants you to make friends. Here you can search through your other social media contacts or look for friends by where you worked and went to school. Facebook will try its best to suggest people you might know.
- **TWO PEOPLE ICON:** This is where you will find friend requests.
- **THE SPEECH BUBBLE:** Here you can read and send messages to other users.
- **THE WORLD ICON:** This is where all of your notifications will pop up. For instance, if someone mentions your name in a post, you will be notified. You will also find replies to your messages and posts, posts from Groups you are following, and Likes you got for your posts
- **PADLOCK ICON:** Here is where you can set who can see your posts and who you'll allow to contact you. This is where you will also find ways to stop people if they are bothering you.
- **DOWN ARROW ICON:** Here is where you go to set up new Pages and Groups, as well as to choose other settings.

THE LEFT-HAND SIDEBAR

Here you will find some of the same links that are in the blue top bar. You will also find Events and your Pages and Groups here. Let's set up a Group now.

Setting Up a Group

Now that you have your account set up, let's look at *Groups*. Groups are communities built around a cause or common Like. Groups can be built for anything that people might have in common—including a genre such as science fiction or fantasy. The content appearing in Groups is community driven, and everyone shares a voice here.

1. Log into Facebook and go to your News Feed. You do this by clicking on the Facebook logo in the top-left corner or by clicking on News Feed under Favorites. This is located in the top-left corner of your Facebook Page.

2. Look for the Groups section in the left-hand bar of the News Feed and then find the Create Group option.

3. Name your group.

4. Invite Facebook members to join your group. (This is optional, of course.)

When you are establishing your Group, Facebook encourages you to draw from your own personal network. Before inviting people to your Group or a Page, let them know ahead of time, as a courtesy. Send them a private message and ask. Most people take offense when added without permission.

1. Choose the Privacy option you want your group to have:

  a. **OPEN:** Anyone can see this Group, who's in it, and what members post.

  b. **CLOSED:** Anyone can see the Group and who's in it, but only members see posts.

  c. **SECRET:** Only members see the Group, who's in it, and what members post.

2. Click on "Create" to establish your Group.

3. Choose an icon to represent your Group.

And your Group is now online. Just a few finishing touches, and you'll be ready to invite and welcome people to this new community.

Completing Your Group's Profile

1. You will be taken to the Group's Page straight away, but in case you aren't, you can type in the name of your Group in the search bar. In the Group's Main Page, find the three periods (...) icon at the right-hand side of the Group's menu and click.
2. Select from the drop-down menu the Edit Group Settings option.
3. Complete the set up your Group.

a. **GROUP NAME:** A custom icon can be assigned to your Group. Your name can be changed, but it is set once your Group grows to more than 250 members.

b. **PRIVACY SETTINGS:** Available only for larger Groups

c. **MEMBER APPROVAL:** Used for moderation of new Group members

d. **GROUP ADDRESS:** An option for establishing a Group e-mail and URL for Facebook.

e. **DESCRIPTION:** Where you offer a greeting and brief description for your group, its aims, its policies, and its dos and don'ts

f. **TAGS:** A great way for Facebook members to easily find you

g. **POSTING PERMISSIONS:** Another moderation option when it comes to the method of posting on the Group board

h. **POST APPROVAL:** Another moderation option when it comes to the method of posting on the Group board

4. Click the Save button.

5. Return to the top of your Group and set an appropriate Group Photo for your welcome banner.

Your Group is now complete, and up and running. All you need are members. On your next few posts that cross the line into business mention that you have a Group and encourage people to join. Even before members join, have a few topics online and ready for discussion.

Starting a Group Topic Discussion

1. Go to your Facebook Group. At the top of your page, just under the introduction banner, you should see this inviting field: Write Post.

2. Click in this field and write the following status message:

> Welcome to my Facebook Group. This is where you will find all news and updates of my upcoming appearances and developments. The rules here are simple: Don't spam, and be excellent to one another. If you cannot do this, one of our moderators will promptly block you from the group. We hope you contribute and adhere to the positive spirit of this Facebook Group.

3. Click on the icon of the camera if you wish to upload an accompanying photo. (If you want to upload a different photo with your message or no photo at all, roll over the image and single-click the X in the top-right corner of the image.)

4. Click the Post button.

The most recent post in your group will appear at the top of your Group. This will always be the case until someone in the Group leaves a comment. The topic with the most recent comment will jump to the top of the posts, taking priority until a new topic is posted or another comment is left elsewhere in the various threads available here.

Note that you can upload photos and videos, ask questions of your Group members in poll fashion, or add a file (PDF, Word document, etc.) to share with your membership. Your content does not need to be just general discussions. As moderator, you can also decide which posts stay and which posts are deleted, and approve or dismiss members.

Therein you have the basics of a Group. Now, what about a Page?

Setting up a Facebook Page

1. Go to your Facebook News Feed or to your Personal Page.
2. Single-click on the downward arrow icon in the upper-right corner and select from the drop-down menu the Create Page option.
3. From the Create a Page introduction page, select the kind of Page you wish to create.

a. The features for each of these options may differ slightly, but the basics—the Admin Panel, Recent Posts by Others, posting options, etc.—are all the same. The options offered by Facebook include Local Business or Place; Company, Organization, or Institution; Brand or Product; Artist, Band, or Public Figure; Entertainment; and Cause or Community.

   b. These options help Facebook categorize what kind of Page you are managing for search purposes.

4. Based on your selection, fill in the appropriate information for your Page. This is a professional page, so share as much information as you deem necessary for conducting business. If this is a home business, do you really want to post your home address? Many authors maintain a private mailbox for this reason.

5. Click the checkbox for Facebook's Terms of Service. Perhaps it is not the most engaging read online, but review Facebook's Terms of Service in order to be clear on what is and isn't allowed, and how your content can (and cannot) be used by Facebook.

6. Click the Get Started button to launch your Page.

7. You will receive an e-mail welcoming you to Pages while you are rerouted to a new website that will walk you through the process of completing a Page's profile. Some of these details can be edited after the Page is live, but complete the options here in order to get the basics up and running.

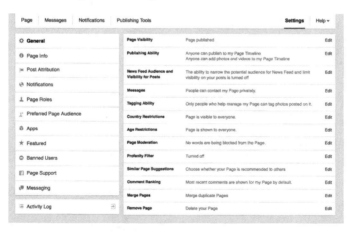

At any time, you can delete a Page by going onto the Page itself. Click on Settings, and at the bottom of the list of settings you will find Remove Page. Click there. Facebook will ask if you really want to re-move it. If you click again, there is no way back, so be sure that's what you want to do.

Now, your new Page is live and running. No one yet knows it's out there, mind you, but we will get into building your Page Following in a moment.

Let's break down a complete page and discuss how to create a unique look, as well as what a quality page looks like.

BOOKMARK

If you have more than one moderator for your Page, it is not a bad idea to end your post with initial signatures. As I do with One-Stop Writer Shop, I moderate this Page with Pip. There-fore, when I make a posting, I will sign it with (TM) so that the reader knows who is posting the item.

Posting on a Page

Here is an example of how to create a simple post to Facebook:

1. Go to your Facebook Page. At the top of your page, just under the header, you should see a field that says: "What have you been up to?"
2. Click in this field and write the following status message:
    > Not all Kickstarter accounts succeed, as Kickstarter is more than just crowdfunding. It is also a place for market testing and hard business lessons. (TM)
3. Hold down the Shift button and then, with the Shift button still down, hit Return twice.
4. In this space, type the following link: http://teemorris.com/2014/03/16/lessons-learned-kickstarter/.
5. Once the link preview appears in the post, select the link and emp-ty space underneath your post, and remove it. This is just a nice

way to clean up posts appearing on your Page in order to avoid double posting a URL. By entering Shift+Return, you do not prematurely make the post live on your Page or in your Feed.

6. Click the Post button.

BOOKMARK

NOTE: If you have liked other Pages, sometimes you are offered options of names, places, and businesses that match up with what you are typing, even without adding the @ to what you are typing.

Sharing a Post

1. On your Page, click on the Share option for a post. When you Share a post on a Facebook Page or in a friend's feed, not only will the post appear in its entirety on your friend's Facebook feed, but a link back to the page of origin will also appear on that feed, offering people a direct connection to your Page.

2. Click in the Post field and begin writing the following status message: *Here's a reminder that @One.* You should see a drop-down menu appear with options for One-Stop pages. From the drop-down menu, select One-Stop Writer Shop from the offered Pages. In the field where you are composing your accompanying post, you will see a highlighted One-Stop Writer Shop link in the field.

3. Finish writing the status message:

   … will be appearing in Richmond two nights after the release of DAWN'S EARLY LIGHT. Pick up your copy, attend the James River Writers' WRITING SHOW, and get it signed!

4. Single-click Share Link to make your post live.

APPENDIX E

Twitter

SETTING UP A TWITTER ACCOUNT

Welcome to the first step in building your Twitter network. Twitter developers want to help you through this process, as you will see when you set up your account.

1. Go to http://twitter.com using your browser.
2. Just underneath the New to Twitter? question, click Sign up.

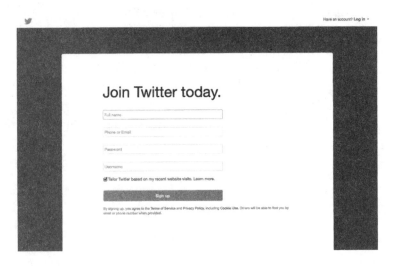

When coming up with a username for your Twitter account, it is a good idea to think *compact* and *easy to type*. Replies on Twitter tend to be shorter for those with longer usernames (defined here as anything over ten characters), as the 140-character limitation does include the username.

3. Enter your name, an e-mail, and a password. Once the fields are complete, single-click the Sign Up for Twitter button.

4. Review what is listed for your Twitter credentials and single-click the Create My Account button.

5. You will be asked to supply a phone number, which you can skip if you like.

6. You will be taken through a process in which Twitter tries to learn more about you by asking you what you are interested in. Then it will try to find followers for you.

7. After this, you will customize your profile, or you can skip this step and come back to it later. But you don't want to remain a Twitter egg for long.

8. Next, Twitter will ask you to find people you know, which you can do using your e-mail contacts. You can also skip this step.

9. Now you will be taken to your home page, with a pop-up prompting you to confirm your e-mail. Do it.

10. If you have followed people in the previous steps, you will see their recent tweets pop up in your feed. A *tweet* is a message shared on the public Twitter stream. The *Twitter stream* shows the incoming messages from your network, and it appears on your public Timeline.

11. Click on the camera icon on your profile and upload a snappy shot of yourself.

12. Your Twitter account is now live and ready to go.

GETTING TO KNOW TWITTER

Welcome to Twitter! You could just head out from here, but there are other little touches that you can add to your Twitter account on your own time, and the following are recommended:

1. To access the details in the above image, go to your Twitter page by clicking on your profile in the top-left corner.
2. Now click on Edit Profile on the left. Here is where you spice up your profile. You should fill in your bio, location (something as simple as your state is fine), and, most important, your website. You can also tweak the theme's color.
3. Don't forget to add a header photo for the space behind your profile picture. This area can be easily customized. Whatever image you place here will be seen by all who pull up your profile, in all Twitter apps.

BOOKMARK

If you have difficulty uploading an image for Twitter, the photo's size or resolution may need to be reduced, or it could be the wrong format. Profile pics must be no larger than 700K and no larger than 600 × 600 pixels in dimension.

Header images should be 1252 × 626 and no larger than 5 MB. Backgrounds can vary, but as they tend to be tiled when smaller than the screen resolution, we recommend using images that are 2000 × 2400. All of these images should be 72 pixels per inch (ppi), saved as either a JPEG or PNG, and use the RGB scale.

TALKING ON TWITTER

So, if you haven't used Twitter before, you're probably thinking "What about that whole 140-characters-or-less limitation? You really can't say a lot, can you?"

This segment is less about unleashing your inner social media geek and more about embracing your inner editor.

Posting Your Tweet

When you have the perfect tweet, what do you do with it? Well, you go on and you release it into the world, of course.

1. Go to Twitter using your Internet browser. If you are logged in and you told Twitter to remember you, you should still be logged in. (If not, go ahead and log in.) Depending on where you are in your Twitter account, you have two places where you can compose your tweet. You can click on the Home icon of your Twitter home page and use the Compose window offered in the left-hand sidebar or click on the quill icon in the upper right of the menu bar to access a separate Compose window.

2. In the Compose New Tweet window, enter in something like the following:

   This is my first tweet. Thanks for the help on this, @1SWShop and @JamesRvrWriters. #rva #masterclass

3. When you have your tweet composed and checked for typos and grammar errors, you are one click away from communicating with your community and with the Twitter network.

4. Single-click the Tweet button. Your screen automatically refreshes, and your message appears at the top of your visible Timeline.

Your message is now out in the Twitterverse for those in your network and (depending on the security you have in place) the Public Timeline to see.

Type. Proof. Post. That's all there is to it!

Now that you are effectively tweeting, the next step is to respond to your first tweet and understand how to talk to another person on Twitter.

Replying to a Tweet

After you post your tweet, someone might tweet back, "Who is Tee Morris, and what does he have to do with Twitter?" but the tweet will appear in your Timeline like this:

> Tee Morris @TeeMonster
> You're taking a master class in Richmond? Where? And who is @1SWShop and @JamesRvrWriters?

This is a reply or a *Notification* on Twitter. A notification begins with a user's avatar, the replier's username, your username preceded by an @ symbol, and finally the tweet. By adding in the @ symbol and username, the mention is recognized by the Twitter home page (and other third-party applications) as a reply to you.

1. Whether you are in the Notifications mode or your Timeline window, find your mention. Single-click on the arrow labeled Reply to open a tweet field.
2. Enter your reply by clicking to the right of the Twitter handles. If you want to mention the other Twitter accounts in your reply, reposition them accordingly. Your reply, after editing, should look like this:

@TeeMonster Tee Morris is one of the @1SWShop founders and @JamesRvrWriters is hosting a Social Media master class.

3. Single-click on the Tweet button.

You'll be notified that your reply was sent. Notifications provide a quick connection to those following you, and you can give an @Mention to anyone on Twitter, even those outside your network.

BOOKMARK

Under Notifications, you will see two available options: *Interactions* and *Mentions*. While Mentions reveals all of the replies your tweets are receiving, *Interactions* is a more thorough look at the activity your Twitter account is experiencing in the network. This mode will also give you indications of who has started following you and when your tweets are *retweeted* across the network. (An explanation of the retweet is coming next.)

Another form of replying is called the retweet. With a single click, you copy another Twitter account's tweet or reply. This kind of response is either preceded by an *RT:* or it appears in your Timeline a second time with the title "Retweeted by [Twitter Handle]" above the original tweet.

1. In your Home Timeline window, find a tweet you want to share in your network. Single-click on the looping arrows labeled Retweet to open a Retweet window.
2. Single-click the Retweet button.

You should notice the Retweet option is now green and reads as retweeted in your Timeline.

Some applications, both desktop and mobile, will offer a second option to *quote* a tweet. This option allows you to add your own commentary into a retweet, if there are available characters remaining. Here's an example:

> @1SWShop "@TeeMonster Tee Morris is the writer of All a Twitter and the teacher of the Social Media Mainline." He knows his stuff!

OR

> @1SWShop RT: @TeeMonster Tee Morris is the writer of All a Twitter and the teacher of the Social Media Mainline. (He knows his stuff!)

By using quotes around what you are retweeting, or parentheses around what you are adding, you make sure to add your own spin on what is being said. Retweets are used to spread a message, a link, or just something really cool throughout the Twitter network.

DIRECT MESSAGES

A feature that has landed a few people in trouble (in that they didn't understand how Twitter operates), and that Twitter has worked hard to make foolproof (although fools still rush in), is the *Direct Message*, or *DM* as it is referred to in the Twitterverse. When you receive @Mentions, you catch them either in your network's Timeline or in your Notifications. Direct Messages are different. DMs are seen by you and only you (unless someone is looking over your shoulder, of course), and are found under *Messages*.

BOOKMARK

Unlike @Mentions, which can be made to anyone in the Twitter network, Direct Message replies can be sent only to people who are following you.

Composing a Direct Message

1. On your Twitter home page, single-click the Messages option, the envelope/speech bubble icon located after the Home and the Notifications icons.
2. Type in the Twitter name of the person you want to send a message to and click Next.
3. In the field at the bottom of the DM window, type in your message:
   Hi there. Thank you for the follow. I love the class so far.
4. Single-click the Send Message button.

The DM you sent appears when you click on the envelope/speech bubble icon. Now the sender has been notified and you simply await a reply. To reply to a DM, the process is even easier.

Replying to a Direct Message

1. On your Twitter home page, check the envelope/speech bubble icon. If a number appears, it means you have unread DMs. Single-click the icon.
2. The conversation will appear. Single-click the unread DM to view the conversation in its entirety.
3. In the field at the bottom of the DM window, type in a reply.
4. Single-click the Send Message button.

Although this is a private means of communication on Twitter, keep in mind that there will be a delay between DMs, as tweets need to find their way through the network. If you need a quicker reply time, it would be a better idea to move the talk to Skype, AIM, or some other chat application. DMs are the best way to have private conversations with someone on Twitter. The messages remain between you and the recipient unless you move out of the DM section and into the public stream.

Also beware of accidentally typing a DM into the public stream. This kind of mistake is often called "DM FAIL." The results can range from the embarrassing to the career breaking, so it never hurts to double-check that you are in fact sending a DM. Many celebrities and politicians have fallen victim to this faux pas, and we want to help writers avoid it.

Google+

SETTING UP A GOOGLE+ ACCOUNT

Google does its best to make things as simple and integrated as possible for its users. Once you have a Google account, you can use it to access Google, Gmail, Chrome, YouTube, Google Maps, Google Play, and, best of all, Google+.

1. Go to https://accounts.google.com/SignUp.
2. Enter the information required. It will let you know if the username you have chosen is already taken.
3. Agree to the terms and service, and click next.
4. You will have to verify your account with an e-mail, text message, or phone call.
5. Enter the verification number.
6. Set up your profile.
7. Click on the blue person icon in the top right-hand corner.
8. You'll be prompted to find people to connect with. You can search for them on Google+ or find friends on Yahoo! or even Hotmail.
9. Google will then ask you to follow things you love; you can either do this now or follow up later.
10. Fill in your profile, giving as much information as you are comfortable sharing—don't forget to mention that you are an author! Use a good, representative picture of yourself, or if you are feeling brave, snap one from your camera.

Your profile is now done, but let's take a tour of the place.

GETTING TO KNOW GOOGLE+

Once you have added people to your Circles, you will begin seeing their content on the Google+ home page. In the top bar, you will see you can filter this stream of content by Circles of friends, family, and others you have set up. It's a nice idea to make Circles for your professional interests: book bloggers, publishers, agents, and such.

On the left, directly below the Google+ logo, is the home icon with a downwards arrow. Hovering over this will bring up a menu of what you can access from here.

Profile

This lets you see your profile how others will see it. It's a good opportunity to consider the public face you are presenting. Click on View Profile As: and change from Public to Yourself. Here is where you can change your cover image, change which Circles you have people in, and add posts. You can share text, pictures, a link, a video, an event, or even run a poll.

People

This page will offer people Suggestions that are based on shared friends or interests that you have in common. Check under Added

You below that. Google+ doesn't send you e-mail alerts when someone adds you, only messages under the bell icon in the top right corner, so these adds can pile up. Be sure to get around to sorting people into Circles, if you accept them, or you may ignore them as necessary. Gmail contacts will run through your Gmail in search of people you already are connected to. Google+ will also try to find more contacts for you, depending on your profession, where you went to school, or where you work. (It is frighteningly accurate with these things.) Finally, you can allow it to connect to your other e-mail accounts so it can hunt for contacts there.

Photos

Here is where you will find, and can upload, all those images you want. It is also where you can find images that you are tagged in.

Collections

Here is where you can group your posts by topic. It makes it easier for your followers who share a particular interest with you to find posts you've made about that interest. Once you've made your first collection, there will be a new tab available where you can access them.

Communities

Like Facebook Groups, Google+ communities are built around shared interests. Google+ will try its best to figure out what communities you might be interested in. It wouldn't hurt to join a few writing-based ones, or you might even create one of your own.

Events

Google+ will search out events from your Circles and place them here. This is also where you can create your own event, such as a book launch, a reading, or a celebration Hangout.

Hangouts

One of the standout features of Google+, Hangouts is where it is happening. Clicking on this link will show you who in your Circles is having a Hangout. It is also the place where you can start a Hangout yourself. Time to get that book group or beta reader session going. Simply click on "Start a Hangout on Air" under "Hangouts on Air," give it a name, and tell people what it is about. You can choose to start one immediately or schedule one for a later date or time. Also, you can select which of your Circles you would like to include. Consider your audience and whether you want to make the Hangout exclusive or for a wider audience.

Pages

Here is where you find the Pages that you've created, and where you can manage them. Click on the Page if you have created one. Now you can add content, get insights into how your Page is doing, and start a hangout for the Page. This is where you can also start a brand-new Page for a new series.

Settings

Here is where you can alter all the setting for your account. Look particularly at the Notifications section and decide how much, and for what, you want Google to notify you about.

Top-Right Bar

The + icon, and/or the home icon, will take you to the stream of information that all of your circles have produced, and you can post information there as well.

The grid of squares will bring up all the additional Google offerings, like Youtube.com, News, Calendar, Drive, Search, Maps, Play, and Gmail. Ain't integration great?

- The bell icon will show you all the notifications, including when you get mentioned and when people have added you to a circle.
- The plus sign in a box is another opportunity for you to post.
- The circle with your avatar is another way to get to your profile and your Pages, and to log out.

Below these icons are two final icons. The two people icon brings up suggestions of people to add, because Google+ needs you to create Circles as soon as possible. The quotation marks in a bubble will bring up recent Hangout information. There you'll see all your previous Hangouts and whether you missed a video call. Remember, by clicking on the down arrow to the right of Hangouts, you can set your mood, status, and notifications for Hangouts. It also lets those in your Circles see when you are online.

YouTube

SETTING UP A YOUTUBE ACCOUNT

If you have a Google Account, you will be presented with a chance to use that account for YouTube. If you do not have one, you will be prompted to create one. Google is trying to integrate all of its different services under one umbrella.

In the realm of social networking, you will be asked a lot of personal information. Rarely will a social networking site ask for details and refuse access if you do not answer all of the data fields. However, the more you can offer potential contacts, the more success you will achieve in building strong communities. Give only as much information as you feel comfortable giving, but make sure you cover the basics: an avatar, your name, where you are, and what you are all about.

Once you have created your Google account, you will have access to all the features YouTube offers.

GETTING TO KNOW YOUTUBE

All you need to do now is upload your video. Before reaching for just any media creation you have on hand, you should know something about what works (and what doesn't) on this video-sharing service. Videos appearing on YouTube must fit certain technical criteria. They must be:

- less than 10 minutes in length
- smaller than 100 MB
- in the format of AVI, MOV, MPG, or WMV

If your video fits this criteria, then you can begin the uploading process.

A site similar to YouTube is *BlipTV* (http://blip.tv). Like YouTube, BlipTV is also free and offers the same ability to share video from blog to blog. The downside is that its compression is much harder than YouTube, meaning the video quality will vary. The upside: There are no limitations. Your videos can be as long as you like.

UPLOADING YOUR VIDEO ON YOUTUBE

Once you have the video criteria met, you can upload your video. You are only a few clicks away from uploading your media to the world's most popular video-sharing service.

1. Click on the Upload button located in the upper-right corner of YouTube's interface.
2. Click on Select File to Upload, and browse your computer to find the video file you want to upload. Select the video file and then single-click on Select to advance to the details page.
3. While the progress bar shows the uploading process, fill in details about the clip that will display on the video's page. Click on the Save Changes button to accept these details.
4. Click the Upload Video button located underneath the current video uploading to place a second video in your uploading queue.

Depending on your connection and YouTube's traffic, the uploading process of your video will wrap up within minutes.

Once the video is online, your content is offered on your YouTube channel. The video will remain embedded on this page until you or YouTube removes it from the server.

YouTube usually removes content from its server when the content violates its terms of service or if it violates copyright. In all other instances, the user will remove content from a YouTube channel.

Now that you have your YouTube account set up and your first video online, let's share this video …

EMBEDDING YOUR YOUTUBE VIDEO IN A BLOG

1. On the video's host page, look for the Embed field located to the right of the YouTube page.
2. Select Share and then Embed. Copy the code below into your clipboard either with CTRL + C (PC) or Command + C (Mac).
3. Go to your WordPress account, then to Posts > Add New, and compose a post that introduces your video clip.
4. After composing a brief introduction, switch composition modes from Visual to HTML and paste into your entry the embed code copies you took care of back in Step 2. When embedding your video, you cannot use the Visual editor, so you'll need to use the Code editor.
5. Click either Save Draft to save the draft for later or Publish to make the post live.

Now you have video incorporated with a blog post, providing other bloggers the ability to distribute your video by sharing the embed code from blog to blog. While the traffic comes from many different locations, all your hits are recorded on YouTube, increasing your visibility for casual YouTube visitors. The site remains the most popular one for online video content and is regarded as the go-to for media sharing sites.

Pinterest

SETTING UP A PINTEREST ACCOUNT

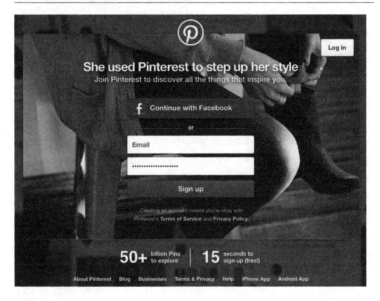

You can log into Pinterest with your Facebook account, but if you don't want to do that, follow these instructions:

1. Supply your e-mail address and create a password.
2. Provide your name, age, and gender.
3. In order to discover your interests, Pinterest has you pick at least five interests to begin with, but you can always add more later on. Click on Follow.

4. Pinterest will now gather Pins it thinks you will be interested in based on those initial choices.

5. Don't forget to confirm your e-mail address.

Settings

Go to your profile. Clicking on the gear icon will bring up your account setting. Here is where you can personalize your Pinterest account. You can set your privacy settings so Google doesn't search your Pins. However, as a writer who's trying to get noticed, you probably don't want to do that—the more ways people can find you, the better. You can decide if you want Pinterest to send you e-mail notifications when someone repins one of your Pins or a selection of other activities. You can also choose to set up your other social media accounts to post when you Pin. Pinterest can post directly to your Facebook Timeline, your Twitter Stream, and your Google+ Page. These settings should be used with caution, however, as you don't want to flood all of your feeds with the same information and risk driving people away.

GETTING TO KNOW PINTEREST

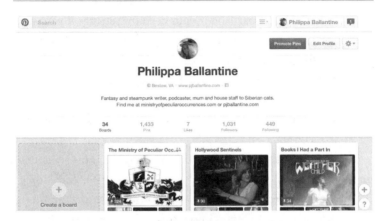

When you first log into Pinterest, you won't see much. Only a few boards will be available, originating from your suggestions as a new pinner, but soon enough you'll be pinning from all over the place. Let's look over the layout.

On the left is the small Pinterest logo. Clicking on this will always bring you back to the home page. Next to the logo is the search bar where you can input keywords to look for items of interest pinned by others. Right next to it is a three-line icon. This will bring up categories you can use to find interesting items.

To the right of that should be your name. Clicking on this will bring you to your boards.

BOOKMARK

If you want to share a board (for instance with a publicist, co-writer, or your personal assistant) then simply go to your board, click Edit Board, and add the e-mail of that person under collaborators. Once she has accepted your invitation, she will be able to pin to your board, and you can set about making magic together ... or at least an interesting board.

On the right now should be your Edit Profile button. Use this if you want to tweak your profile in any way after the initial setup.

Next to that, the gear icon is your account settings if you want to change your original setup. If you have converted your personal account into a business one (see Chapter 8), then this is where you will access your analytics information. It's also the place to create widget code to place into your own Web page. Finally, you can also log out here, but that's not something you have to do unless you have multiple accounts.

Back in the main page, the last icon next to your name is a double-pin icon. This is where you access News (what other people are doing), You (what other people are doing with your information, repinning, liking, and also anyone you know through other networks who has just joined Pinterest), and Messages. Unlike some other media platforms, you're not likely to get too many messages, but do keep an eye on it.

Finally, and most important, the bottom left of the page is a plus symbol. This is where you can upload images directly, or from the Web, and create another board. Remember, while a Pin is an image or video, a board is a collection of Pins. Keep that kitchen corkboard in mind and it'll be easy to remember.

Now that we've had a quick tour of the Pinterest neighborhood, let's see what we can do with it.

WORKING WITH PINTEREST

Like all of the social networks, the key is community. Luckily, Pinterest makes it very easy to go out and find your community.

First of all, search "authors," "writers," or "[insert your genre here] books." You can choose to follow the boards you find, but if you check a little deeper into the owner of the board, you might find other common interests. You can chose to follow all or just some of their boards.

As we said in earlier chapters, don't just stick with your colleagues. Broaden those horizons! Find people who share other interests with you as well. The most popular Pins on the site are cooking and dining, DIY and crafting, health, funny stories, beauty and fashion, and technology.

Find some boards and pinners that you find interesting and follow away. If you do so, your Pin stream will be full of interesting pictures and videos. These are great resources for repinning.

When you click on a Pin, it will become much larger, and if you click again, if there is a link, you will be taken to that site. Or you can simply click on the Visit Site button for the same effect.

It's a good idea to check links, because some less moral pinners might try a bait-and-switch—or the link might have been removed or moved. Remember, you want to provide your audience with great content, so it's worth it to take a moment to examine what you are repinning.

Repinning is a great way to enhance your feed and the community, and to pad how often you are marketing those books of yours.

It really is very simple. When you hover over other people's Pins, you hit the Pin It button. Then you have a choice of which board you want to Pin to and whether you want to add a description.

As on other social media platforms, commentary is a good idea here. You can put the original information in some square brackets and then put your comment before or after that. In this way, you preserve the original pinner's words, which makes you a good community member. Your comments can be as simple as "I'm going to try and make these muffins!" or "This looks like a dress my heroine in [insert my title here] would wear."

BOOKMARK

It is always good Pinterest etiquette to credit your sources if you can. Also, using other people's images but linking to your blog or Web page is an underhanded practice and can inspire people to leave negative comments. Don't do it if you want to develop a good Pinterest reputation.

If you have a contact on Pinterest who you think would really appreciate a particular Pin, you can send it directly to that person. Use this feature with caution, and never try and spam people with your Pins!

Finally, there is the Heart button, which is similar to the Like button on Facebook. Commentary and repinning is the nicest way to show appreciation, but if it doesn't fit in with any of your boards, this is a way to give the original pinner a thumbs up.

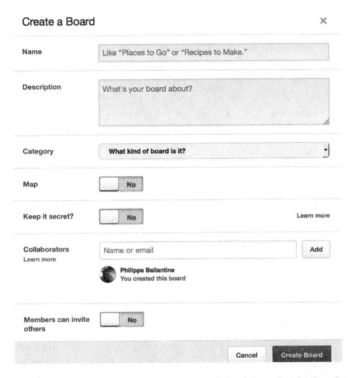

Creating boards on Pinterest is easy, and don't be afraid of making too many. The more boards, the more interests, and the more views. From your profile, click on the large gray plus sign with Create a Board. From here give your board a name and a description, and find a category it fits into. Map will create a map, which will link to Pins—this is a great idea if you board is travel themed. You can also choose to make the board secret or not. Secret boards, as we talked about in Chapter 8, are great for saving items to Pin later, or for boards about projects you're not quite ready to talk about yet. You can also add collaborators and choose if they can add new members to this board themselves.

Uploading a Pin of Your Own

Now to the exciting stuff. Let's add some content of your own. Book covers, fan art, images of people you'd like to see play your characters, places where you have set your stories—all of these make excellent uploads.

1. Click on the plus icon and choose the image from your computer. It can be a GIF, JPEG, or PNG file. Choose the board you want to add it to, or create a new board for this image ... but only if it fits in with your interests. Too many boards with only a few images are not enticing.
2. The important part of this Pin is the description. Keep in mind what your readers might be looking for. Include a substantial description about what this image means to you.
3. Don't forget a couple of hashtags, and if it is relevant, now is the time to insert a link. The link should, at the very least, lead back to your website; if not, link to a location where the all-important impulse buy can be made.

Finally, if you have connected other social networks, you can choose to post it there.

There—you've done it. You have your first original Pins!

APPENDIX I

Instagram

SETTING UP AN INSTAGRAM ACCOUNT

Getting an account together on Instagram is quite easy, provided you have the app loaded onto your smartphone. Instagram is available on iOS (iPhone), Android, and Windows, and runs on all varieties of smartphones.

First, download and install Instagram onto your smartphone from the App Store for your device.

1. Launch Instagram on your phone. Your options for establishing an Instagram account include using your Facebook credentials or your e-mail. Use whichever method works best for you. The steps we outline here apply to using an e-mail to register your Instagram account.

2. Tap Register with E-mail, and on the next screen, enter the following:

a. a username (the nickname you want to go by on Instagram)

b. a password

c. a valid e-mail address

3. Tap the Photo icon in the center of the screen and select a photo (or take a new one) for your profile picture. Choose one that best represents you as an author.

4. Tap the arrow pointing right to follow validation steps (which requires you to reply via e-mail) to finish your profile.

The *profile*, like other profiles you will find online, is the place where you can introduce yourself. You can edit this content at any time from your account or from the app by tapping on the profile icon on the far right of the menu bar and then tapping the Edit Your Profile option.

GETTING TO KNOW INSTAGRAM

Now your account is ready to go, so let's check out some of the features.

First off, you will see immediately that Instagram is not designed as a desktop app but more for "capturing it instantly" through your smartphone. (Now the name makes sense, right?) In fact, you cannot upload photos or video from your computer—all your Instagram posting has to be done through your phone.

BOOKMARK

Another terrific way to track popular tags on Instagram is by allowing the website Statigram[1] access to your Timeline. Statigram allows you to look up photos through hashtags in a gallery-style format, unlike Instagram, which allows you to look up hashtags one account at a time. Other options that Statigram offers include account statistics, enhanced comment postings, and network maintenance.

---

1 http://statigr.am

Take a look at the menu bar running along the bottom of Instagram. These five icons are all the options you need to get around the Instagram app, build your Instagram network, and interact with others. From left to right, your icons are as follows:

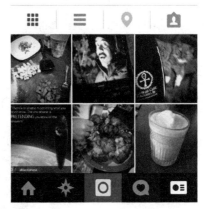

- **HOME:** The *Home* icon takes you to your Timeline of Instagram users. Their posts will appear here. You will also see an inbox icon, which is where you can send and receive direct messages.
- **EXPLORE:** If you want to check out and follow popular accounts on Instagram, search for users you might know, or look up hashtags people are attaching to their images, you can do all this in the *Explore* option by tapping on the compass rose icon.
- **CAMERA:** When you are ready to take a photograph with Instagram, tap the camera icon. Depending on your preferences, your screen will be divided into thirds (a photographer's trick for framing up your subject), or it will provide just a clear view from the lens. Tapping on the screen will establish what you want the focus point of the photo to be. You can also flip the camera around for *selfies* (self-portraits), choose a *flash mode*, and switch to *video mode* (the icon to the right) or back to *still camera mode* (the icon to the left). The center button can take photos (when blue) or shoot video (when red).

- **NOTIFICATIONS:** The speech bubble with the heart is where you go to receive and track *Notifications.* There are two modes here: *Following* and *News.* Keep your Notifications on News in order to see who's following you and to track who Likes your photos.
- **PROFILE:** This final icon is where you can edit your profile. Once in your profile, edit your Preferences by tapping the gear icon in the top-right corner of your smartphone. This option also lets you find out what photos you've been tagged in.

Let's jump right in and start taking photos with Instagram. More important, let's look at how we can take a photograph with the app and then share the photo across a number of social networks.

TAKING A PHOTO ON INSTAGRAM

1. Tap on the Camera icon and take a photo.
2. You can now apply some of the various filters Instagram offers. There are quite a few of them, and you can have a lot of fun trying to find the best one for your image. Instagram lets you see exactly how the photo will look with the filter applied before you commit to it.
3. Tap the far-left icon, the Straighten tool. Place and hold your finger on the Adjustment wheel and rotate the image either right or left. Then tap Done to return to the Edit mode.

4. With the Border option, you can determine whether you want your image to have a border (blue) or no border (white).
5. The Blur option offers three modes:

   a. None (white),
   b. Circle (blue drop with circle), and
   c. Bar (blue drop with bar).

6. Tap each mode to decide where you want the blur and which design works best for your image.
7. Lux allows you to adjust the contrast in the photo. Tap to make adjustments, and then tap Done to return to the original image.
8. Tap Next to enter the Share mode, or tap the left arrow at the top of the screen to return to Photo Edit mode.

the appeal of instagram is taking a simple image and getting creative with it. After applying filters and effects on this image, you can then post on Instagram, and on Facebook and Twitter as well. It gives amateurs the chance to have some fun with photographs.

Now we have to share this image through our social networks.

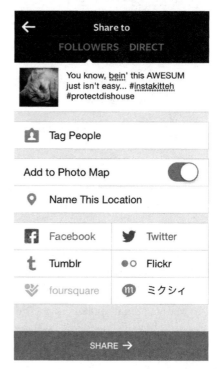

1. In Instagram's Share to mode, compose a caption for the photo. Don't forget that there are two kinds of sharing in Instagram: *Followers* and *Direct*. Followers are open posts on your network. Direct messages are

similar to DMs on Twitter. Images and video shared in Direct mode allow you to share with select members of your network.

2. Add two hashtags related to your photo, then tap OK in the upper-right corner of the screen. The *Tag People* option is best used only after your network is up and running. This is how you can tag friends who appear in the image. Notification of tagging appears under your *Profile* option.

3. Now tap Name This Location to tag your location.

4. If you are tagging your location, leave Add to Photo Map turned on. Some people do not like others to know where they are or where they have been. Use your own discretion on this.

5. There are eight social networks you can connect to your Instagram:

    a. Facebook
    b. Twitter
    c. Tumblr
    d. Flickr
    e. Foursquare
    f. Mixi (Japan)
    g. Weibo (China)
    h. NKontakte (Russia)

6. Tap each network where you want to share this image.

7. If you have not connected your networks to Instagram, you will be walked through a log-in process. You will only have to make this connection once.

8. Tap Share to post your image.

There you go! You will see your image appear instantly on your Instagram Timeline; if you also tapped *Facebook* and *Twitter* before tapping the Share feature, you have effectively shared your image across three networks in one post.

Many popular applications—Pinterest, YouTube, Yelp, Starbucks, Vivino, and Untappd, for example—allow for multiplatform posting like this. The networks offered may differ from app to app, but Facebook and Twitter are often offered as posting platforms.

Instagram is one such app that is popular among apps for its artistic capabilities, its ease of use, and its engaging content generated for Facebook and Twitter.

BOOKMARK

Instagram can post on Facebook accounts but not on Pages accounts. To put Instagram postings on Pages, you will need to share them from your personal account to your Page.

Index

brands and branding
  on blogs, 16
  and content marketing, 11, 168
  damaging, 176, 184–185, 190–191, 194, 196
  developing, 147–149, 157, 169, 171–173, 176, 190, 198
  on Facebook, 3, 62
  on Google+, 89–90
  on Instagram, 134
  on Pinterest, 113
  on Tumblr, 212, 216
  on Twitter, 3, 73–77, 86
  on YouTube, 103, 106, 109
  on your website, 168

cables, 224
calendar, for planning, 175–176
Camtasia video editor, 102, 106
Carriger, Gail, 55
Cass, Kiera, 36
chat shows, 7
cliffhangers, 161
CommaFeed, 16
comments. *See* reader comments
competitions
  on Instagram, 135–136
  on Pinterest, 115–116
Contact Me/Us section, 15
content
  creating, 205–206
  deciding what to post, 165–178
  evergreen, 19
  original, 38–39
  producing for blogs, 18–21, 36–37
  quality, 12, 68, 70, 179–180
  repurposing, 19
  sources for, 170–172
  syndication of, 28–29
  unethical sharing of, 69
content marketing, 11–13, 165–167
  content to look for, 169–172
  on Facebook, 68–70
  as a promotion tool, 168–169
  questionable use of, 172–3
cover photos
  on Facebook, 62
  on Google+, 90

See also header photos
crowdfunding, 135
Curry, Adam, 7

data mining, 197
Day, Felicia, 95
Disqus, 34
Distiller, 146–149
Drake, Piper J., 150

Easter eggs, 54
editorial calendar, 175–176
enclosure tag, 7
Enole, Megan, 149
"The Evil That Befell Samson" (Ballantine), 54

Facebook, 57–58
  About section, 63
  analytics, 81
  boosting posts on, 66–68
  completing the Group's profile, 231–233
  connecting with Instagram, 127
  content marketing on, 68–70
  embedding page links, 65–66
  getting to know Facebook, 228–229
  Groups, 59–61
  Like my Page posts, 65
  Like option, 63–67
  News Feed, 61
  Pages, 61–64
  Post section, 63–64
  profile picture and cover photo, 62
  scheduling posts, 81
  setting up an account, 226–228
  setting up a Facebook Page, 234–237
  setting up a Group, 229–231
  starting a Group topic discussion, 233–234
  syncing with Instagram, 35
  for writers, 58–68
Facebook parties, 10, 185–188
feedback, 15, 49
Final Cut Pro X, 100
Flickr, 57
  connecting with Instagram, 127–128
Flipboard, 16
followers, purchasing, 10, 68, 193–194
FontKiller 2, 21